5 Mistakes Parents Make

5 Mistakes Parents Make

And Other Modern Parenting Challenges

Dr Anubha Majithia

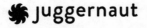

JUGGERNAUT BOOKS
C-I-128, First Floor, Sangam Vihar, Near Holi Chowk,
New Delhi 110080, India

First published by Juggernaut Books 2021

10 9 8 7 6 5 4 3 2 1

P-ISBN: 9789353451523
E-ISBN: 9789353451530

Typeset in Adobe Caslon Pro by R. Ajith Kumar, Noida

Printed at Thomson Press India Ltd

To my parents, Alka and Anil Dhal –
my reason for Being, Belonging and Becoming . . .

Contents

Contents

Author's Note

The word 'parenting' comes from the Latin verb *'parere'*, which means to bring forth. As parents, we continuously strive to bring forth positive experiences into our child's life so that s/he may thrive and become successful in all arenas of life. In this quest for success, parents often develop the 'Fear of Messing Up' (FOMU) and start seeking reassurance through comparisons with other parents and children. These comparisons become an albatross around the necks of both parents and children over time and foster a feeling of 'not being good enough'. Viewing parenting through the monochromatic lens of 'good' or 'bad' is restrictive and rigid as there is no perfect parent or child or 'perfect way to parent a child'. On the contrary, parenting is the confluence of the unique sets of abilities and experiences that parents and children continually bring forth over the years. The success of parenting lies in accepting that mistakes are a part of the process and viewing them as a springboard for growth.

With globalization pervading every aspect of our lives, parenting has also become a melting pot of a variety of practices borrowed from across cultures. The modern Indian parent seeks to imbibe best practices from across the globe and tailor them to his/her needs and circumstances. A balanced approach to parenting involves keeping the traditional cultural practices and value systems as the foundation, and building on it with new blocks of knowledge derived from parenting practices from different cultures. These blocks can be replaced and readjusted as the toddler grows into a young child, who in turn blossoms into an adolescent and then into a young adult.

Parents today are constantly multitasking on many fronts and seek crisp and concise pointers for their concerns. This book has been put together with the aim to provide simple and practical tips that can be easily understood and implemented. It draws from my experiences as a clinical psychologist and a mother of two. The parenting strategies suggested in this book help to improve the ABC central to the holistic and healthy development of a child. 'A' refers to helping parents and the child learn how to manage their 'Affect' or emotions effectively. 'B' refers to promoting productive 'Behaviour' and 'C' refers to fostering positive 'Cognitions' or thoughts. These three aspects are interlinked and influence one another. For instance, teaching an adolescent to counter negative thoughts can aid him/her in curbing anxiety and becoming more focused on the tasks at hand.

In addition to imparting useful parenting strategies, the book also focuses on addressing the importance of mental health for both parents and children. With stress being an integral part of our lives, it is vital that we prioritize our mental health. Seeking professional help should be seen as a sign of insight and strength, rather than as an indication that there is something wrong with us. Just like one needs a trainer to achieve fitness goals, or a tutor at times to support a child academically, a therapist can teach you ways in which you can help yourself and your child better. Children are vicarious learners and observe the ways in which parents react and respond to others and situations. If you as a parent are aware of your thoughts, feelings and actions, and are committed to learn ways to manage each of them effectively, your child will follow suit. I wish this book will give the reader hope that there is light throughout the parenting tunnel.

Dr Anubha Majithia

1

5 Mistakes Parents Make

Regular jobs are easy. They come with a contract which defines the terms and conditions. There are parameters for promotions, perks and bonuses. If at any point you feel it's not your cup of tea, you can always quit and find another. Parenting, on the other hand, is a job like no other. The terms and conditions are subject to change. Appraisals are a daily process and the bosses (the children and society) are difficult to please. Quitting is usually not an option and there is no retirement age. So despite the ante being so high, why do so many take up this job with such fervour?

Wordsworth was on to something when he penned the immortal phrase 'child is the father of man'. Children are a true reflection of their parents and, most often, the parenting experience. As parents, caught up in the web of time, desires and obligations, we find ourselves trapped in the maze of challenges posed to us by our children. Using the age-old method of trial and error, we keep banging against the walls of the maze, only to wonder 'where did we go wrong?' or 'why me?'

I recently attended a school admissions orientation at my daughter's preschool in Noida. The admissions here are based on a blend of background (family income check, degrees check), responsiveness of the child (move over Einstein, my two-year-old can parrot a nursery rhyme, ace logical reasoning and take only one sweet offered by the teacher) and parenting strategy (all those lies about how I don't show my child the screen). So here I was, a second-time parent in the admissions game. I have experienced it all. I represent the minority in the sea of anxious parents, eagerly tuned into the pearls of wisdom being shared by the principal. The thing that amuses me most in the principal's lecture and gets the maximum inter-parent nudging are the questions posed by the school to parents. They range from 'what qualities would you want to inculcate in your child?' to 'what is your parenting mantra?'. While enjoying the admissions circus, I wonder to myself, if only we would reflect on these questions from an introspective lens rather than a materialistic one, we would ace the parenting maze with ease.

Realizing that introspection may be a utopian concept in the age of 'click it to get it', I wonder if we can ace the maze without banging against the walls or giving up. I have my aha moment as I help my six-year-old-son solve a maze. He has a habit of starting the maze and then getting frustrated each time he hits a dead end, to the point of giving up. So I tell him about the secret to cracking any maze – start from the finish line and trace your finger back to the start. The smile on his face as he drags his pencil across the finish line is priceless. If we apply the same logic to the parenting maze, the finish line at any stage is simply a happy child who is able to adapt well to people and circumstances. The walls or dead ends in the maze are akin to the challenges that parents face and the mistakes they make.

1. **One-upmanship**
   This is the first classic mistake parents make. It begins as early as conception. While parents-to-be start competing with each other about the gynaecologist they are visiting and bragging about normal deliveries, young parents show off the school their child is attending and then his/her academic and co-curricular achievements. Ageing parents find pride in boasting about the job and position their child has achieved. Not to be underestimated, one-

upmanship is like a plague and afflicts children from a young age. They too start comparing things like cars and holidays with their peers. Just like termites, one-upmanship eats away at the self-esteem and self-worth of children, leaving them feeling stressed. Rather than keeping up with the Joneses, it is important to first realize your strengths so that you don't confuse self-worth with materialism. Children often vicariously model themselves on their parents, and hence, it is important for parents to derive a sense of self-esteem from abilities rather than liabilities. Moreover, if a parent is able to stand apart from the crowd and embrace the life s/he leads with ease, the child will also develop the confidence to take decisions which play on her/his strengths instead of being based on popular opinion.

2. The price of happiness

This is closely associated with one-upmanship. It is the tendency of parents to please the child with material objects. Parents start buying all sorts of experiences for their children – theme birthday parties, holidays and hobby classes. They seldom realize that the message they send out to the children from an early age is 'happiness can be bought at a price' rather than 'the best things in life are free'. The child from a young age is brought up like a 'little emperor', who summons the parent genie, who in turn responds with 'your whims are my command'. Since the kids have never heard the word 'no', they often feel rejected and have trouble forming healthy relationships.

This leads to children facing adjustment problems right from the time they enter playschool or formal school to later in life. They derive their sense of self from material objects rather than their abilities, which leaves them feeling adrift each time they aren't able to buy their way through life.

3. **Scheduling**

We love to ape the West in all aspects, so the third mistake stems from a concept that is celebrated in the West. Scheduling or keeping the child busy all the time is the new fad. Parents start with scheduling the infant's or toddler's feeding and nap times, and then get addicted to the 'scheduling drug' for life. Children as young as twelve to eighteen months are put into structured programmes at playschools, and then into all sorts of hobby classes. The child returns home exhausted and sleeps early, which is a big win for the parent. There are classes for everything from storytelling to learning how to work the hula hoop.

For some parents, who have long working hours, it is a healthier alternative than keeping the child with a helper. However, for others, it's an excuse for claiming 'me time' or showing off the number of classes the child attends and how talented s/he is to friends and peers (read one-upmanship yet again!).

Whatever the reason, overstimulation and overscheduling are not healthy practices. The definition of intelligence has also been revolutionized and is all about adapting and being flexible (not rigid). Overscheduled children find it difficult to adjust to new situations and get stressed out easily. Too many activities overstimulate the child and shut off the ability to think divergently or creatively. It also feeds into the 'tiger parent' or 'helicopter parent' syndrome, where the parent seeks to control every minute of the child's life, stifling their ability to be independent. While schedules may help in disciplining a child, moderation, flexibility and syncing activities with the child's interests are vital in helping him/her develop into a confident, creative and resilient adult. The child's day needs to have intervals for 'free play' to help her/him become more creative in problem-solving and keeping anxiety at bay.

4. **Quality time**

   Closely linked to the concept of scheduling and making every moment count is the fourth mistake of spending quality time. Millennial parents love this term. It pops up in conversations, parenting advice and admission interviews. Parents love to highlight that quality trumps quantity in every aspect of life, including the time they spend with their child. Quality time translates to the time you give your full attention to the child and are engaged in a goal-directed activity. It is the equivalent of comfort food for the guilty parent who doesn't have 'quantity time'.

   Time is all that children need. They often find it comforting to just have a parent around them and not necessarily engage with them. Instead of quality time, it is important to have 'silly time' – when you aren't involved in any goal-directed or cerebral activity with the child. Parents will be amazed by how children communicate the most interesting things and also their anxieties while just doodling and talking about random things. Parents often choose activities for their children based on societal opinions. Rarely do they pay attention to what the child may like or have an aptitude for. Silly time allows the parent to enter the child's world and learn a lot about him/her. It can provide vital cues about how to communicate with a child in a way that he/she will listen and be more open to. It also sets a foundation for later relationships in a child's life and allows him/her to form open communication channels with the parent, regardless of the age s/he is at.

5. Negative communication
Speaking of communication, the fifth mistake is all about negative communication. As young parents, the first important mode of communication is emotion. When parents respond positively, it propels a child to keep repeating a particular behaviour. Instead of harnessing the power of positive communication, parents easily fall into the trap of negative communication. They find themselves saying 'no' more than 'that's great'. They also point out the negatives more than the positives on a daily basis. I often conduct a small experiment when parents bring children and adolescents with behavioural problems for a therapy session. After listening to their vivid description of everything wrong with their child, I ask them about the things

they feel the child does well. The look on their faces is priceless. As they struggle to think and come up with positives, they learn an important lesson – learn to appreciate before you criticize. Children mostly get attention from parents when they are engaged in negative behaviour as positive behaviour is taken for granted. This encourages kids to engage in negative patterns unconsciously. By shifting the focal point from negative to positive, parents can motivate children to engage in more positive behaviour.

Positive communication as a strategy is not limited to parenting and works wonders with all kinds of relationships – personal or professional.

As we focus on the mistakes we make as parents, it is important to understand that patterns don't break in a day. For any changes that we envisage in our lives and that of our children, we need to be consistent. Another aspect to be mindful of is to forgive yourself each time you make a mistake and own it. More importantly, forgive your child and inculcate patience. Harbouring negativity based on one thing through the day is the worst thing you can do to yourself as a parent and to your child, who often doesn't understand why the punishment has extended throughout the day. No matter how many times you hit roadblocks or dead ends, you always have an option to take a step back, reflect and chart out another path. If you don't give up on yourself, your child won't give up on you!

2

The 3 Ps of Modern Parenting

Move over 'roti, kapda, makaan', parents' fascination with pushing their children to find the 'perfect profession' is here to stay! Even the first conversations with a young child are centred around 'what do you want to be when you grow up?' The trophy wife has long been replaced with the trophy child, whose school, achievements and later professional choices and accolades serve as the show-off element in any social conversation. The result of this circus is pervasive anxiety and flimsy self-esteem, which follows the child and young adult like a shadow, waiting for the other shoe to drop.

The race for the perfect profession starts with the school, or rather the mother–toddler programmes or playschools. Parents want it all – dance, music, art and craft, animation, the works. Even though we seek unconventional schools for our children so they may have a well-rounded personality, the brass tacks of schooling are always marks. Marks ensure admission to the right universities, which yield lucrative campus placements.

The other day I was waiting at the entrance of the playschool that my daughter attends. In between mundane conversations about the heat and children falling sick, my eyes wandered to the bulletin board which read, 'You may be preparing your child for the rat race, what if he is a lion!' The words stuck with me.

As a psychologist, I am intrigued by what makes people tick and what makes them happy. Could the very equation that *societal norms + parental expectations = perfect profession* be faulty? Could the corporate employee who traded her full-time job to become a part-time baker, or the maid who traded her broom for the ladle to a successful tiffin business, have the answer to the age-old riddle of choosing the perfect profession? At a time when age and gender are being defied to break the glass ceiling, and trading the old for new is the norm, a revolution in choosing the perfect profession is the need of the hour. Rather than 'pushing' your child, it is important to celebrate your child.

Reflecting on the psychological mantras that I have become acquainted with over the years, the simple formula for choosing the perfect profession for your child is:

Personality + Potential + Passion = Perfect Profession

- **Personality**, simply defined, is identifying your child's core strengths and being aware of her/his limitations. We often resort to questionnaires/tests to find out what kind of people we are, but this can be done without undergoing such a laborious process. Take a pen and paper and start making a list of your child's abilities, adding the smallest of achievements. Now note down her/his limitations or areas that require improvement. Add a small note about whether you can change them. This small exercise will help us to see that the abilities usually outweigh the limitations.

  This sets the stage for positivity and self-esteem. This small activity is useful in identifying your child's interests and abilities from a young age, paving the path for choosing the perfect profession. Each profession comes with its own skill set that is a blend of abilities. These can be matched with one's unique abilities to help narrow down potential professions.

- After identifying potential professions, it is important to reflect on the **Potential** of those professions and evaluate whether they will further your child's personal and professional growth. Personal growth is facilitated by having a profession which gives you time to indulge in other aspects of your life such as maintaining a stable family and social life and pursuing other interests and, most importantly, solitude.

  Professional growth is not akin to the position or pay package that you may have. It is the blend of job satisfaction and future challenges which nurture diversity and creativity. It is important to stress that profession (or for young children, accolades/marks, etc.) is just a part of the total self. Our lives have various facets and aspects. If a facet or aspect is taking up more that 15 to 20 per cent of your time, then it is time to re-evaluate and come up with a strategy to strike a balance.

- While personality and potential usually ensure material satisfaction, the key to job satisfaction lies in **Passion** – the strong drive which keeps one engaged.

  The world today is a melting pot of professions. Out-of-the-box professions, which may have been taboo in the past, are celebrated with full gusto now. You can be a personal shopper, comedian, rapper and have it all. Passion gives rise to creativity, which goes hand in hand with divergent thinking or the ability to see possibilities in adversity. If you are passionate about a profession, then it will never feel like a 'job to be done', thereby ensuring perseverance towards achieving goals, both professional and personal. Passion is the one aspect of our lives that is not defined by age. Even after you retire from your core profession, your passion for telling stories can lead you in the direction of becoming a professional storyteller!

We live in the world of 4Ds and 4Gs, where the number four has taken precedence over the number three, so I am compelled to add the fourth P to the equation – **Positivity**. In the words of the author and motivational speaker Zig Zigler, 'It is not the aptitude but the attitude that determines your altitude.'

Developing a positive attitude towards your challenges as a parent and helping your child embrace the positives within him/her is the secret to creating the 'perfect family life'.

Perfection is not the utopian concept of being flawless but more about accepting flaws and celebrating yourself, and most importantly about 'following your bliss'!

3

10 Parenting Resolutions

As parents we find ourselves grappling with new challenges on a day-to-day basis, and year after year we are faced with the same dilemma of 'what can I do differently?' The new year brings with it numerous possibilities. It allows us to reflect on the year gone by – what we were able to do well and where we fell short. Just like festivals and celebrations, the new year brings with it the special tradition of making resolutions. Resolutions allow us to translate our will into action and improve ourselves as individuals and parents. Just like a walking buddy makes you more committed to walking daily, making resolutions into a family activity has numerous benefits. First, it helps in teaching children the importance of setting realistic goals and following through with them. Second, it is a great way by which family members motivate each other to stay on track and translate their resolve into action.

To make New Year resolutions a fun-filled family activity, ask each family member to think about five to ten things that they would like to experience or change. Now clearly write them on a piece of paper. To make the list more attractive for children, you can use pictures or ask the child to draw instead of writing out the resolutions to make it look like a vision board. Images often have greater power to invoke positive emotions, which are key to staying motivated to translate the resolve into action. You can have resolutions pertaining to self-improvement and some that involve effective parenting strategies.

Here is a list of ten parenting resolutions which can make this year a happier and healthier experience for your family and you:

- **Family rules**
  The things that parents often struggle with is disciplining their children and sticking to schedules. The problem is that we are busy making children follow the schedule while we slacken every now and then. Writing down family rules helps to voice the expectations we have of each other and keep a check on each other if we slacken. Include your children

when putting down the family rules so that they can be a part of the process and contribute to the list as well. Remember to keep the list simple and achievable so that everyone can follow through with it. You can revise the family rules list every year to renew your resolve.

- **Appreciate before you criticize**

  If our child does something right, we often overlook it thinking that s/he ought to do so, but when s/he falters, we are often quick to reprimand the child and say, 'I won't talk to you,' to add to the guilt. If you want your child to be receptive, start the conversation by appreciating the things that s/he does well to get her/his attention and then talk about what you would like her/him to change. Follow it up by telling the child that you trust her/him to be more responsible in the future. As you learn to appreciate the small things your child does, make it a habit to appreciate others too. It will allow the child to do so as well and imbibe the skill of focusing on people's strengths rather than their weaknesses. This year make it a point to appreciate your child for the small things.

- **Be spontaneous**

  Out of all the memories that I cherish with my son, the ones where we just grabbed an ice cream on the spur of the moment stand out. Everyone likes a surprise and you don't need to look for a special day to plan one. While it is important to follow schedules and be disciplined, it is also important to let your hair down once in a while. It can be as simple as an impromptu picnic or picking up your child from school (for working parents). Being spontaneous fosters the art of thinking creatively or divergently, which propels a person to be a problem-solver rather than a fatalist. So make sure you have many spontaneous experiences.

- **Be more expressive**

  We love to play the game of 'guess what I am thinking of' or 'guess what I want' with our partners and at times with our kids as well. The key to fulfilling relationships lies in good communication. Being expressive and communicating your expectations, likes and dislikes helps people understand each other better. Children learn vicariously, so if you as a parent are more expressive, the child learns to articulate his/her emotions better and also learns the art of being assertive. In addition to being more expressive verbally, don't shy away from giving a warm hug and kiss to your child from time to time. It helps to make the child feel more secure and loved. It is a myth that children do not need a hug beyond a certain age. Resolve to be more expressive about your likes and dislikes and let the hugs keep rolling in.

- **Embrace an active and organic lifestyle**
  The one thing which amuses me every time I go out is drivers stopping the car right in front of a school gate to drop and pick up kids and aunties getting off in front of the shop in busy markets, oblivious to the nuisance caused. We teach our children from an early age that the maid is to be called on for a glass of water and fast food is the epitome of a celebration, resulting in our minds becoming dull and bodies becoming slaves to obesity and diseases. Making a commitment to get your family, especially your child, to engage in physical activity and opting for organic and healthy eating options is the first step to ensuring a healthy and happy future. Make a commitment to eating healthier and being more active as a family in the coming year.

- **Giving back**
  We encourage children to be independent from a very young age, but seldom do we stress on them becoming dependable. Rather than just celebrating a birthday at an orphanage, encourage your children

to commit to a cause. It can be anything from planting a tree to volunteering at an animal shelter or teaching street children. You can serve as a model for your children as well by embracing a cause and making your child a part of the experience. If children learn to extend themselves beyond the self, they are less likely to feel depressed or lonely. An attitude of giving back also inculcates a sense of being grateful about so many things that we take for granted. At times these endeavours can also unlock a passion that your child may have for a cause that can be taken up as a profession. So help your child pick a cause that s/he can commit to for the year.

- **Limit setting**
  The secret to being an effective parent is to emulate a potter who supports the clay with one hand and beats it into shape with the other. Setting limits is an important part of disciplining the child and teaching him/her how to take direction and strike a balance between indulgence and responsibility. The first step to setting limits can be drawing up a list of what is acceptable and what is not. For younger children, who are more visual, you can put up a chart of pictures for the same. You can also get children to draw or colour those pictures to be

able to internalize the limits that are being set. For teenagers, you can discuss what is negotiable and what is not negotiable with them. Being consistent about the limits and boundaries is equally important as consistency sets the stage for constancy. Make a resolve to set limits for your child and follow through with them.

• **Engage in an activity together**
Every child has a special talent/ability. To really bond with a child, it is important to spend time with him/her and get to know what s/he loves to do. Take out a few minutes from your day and engage in an activity with your child. It can be racing toy cars with a toddler or watching a television show with your teenager. Resolve to start with just ten minutes a day to do an activity with your child.

• **Accept your child as s/he is**
We often fall into the trap of comparing our children with each other or with other children. Our conversations also start with 'I wish s/he was like ...' or 'I wish s/he did ...' This percolates into the child's psyche and if s/he commits a mistake or falls short of expectations, s/he hides it or feels

guilty. Not feeling accepted or not being able to live up to parental expectations at times pushes children towards the abyss of depression or suicide. Hence, it is important for parents to communicate acceptance more than desires. You can always communicate to the child that you would like him/her to work towards improving certain aspects and that you are aware that at times s/he may fail. Reinforce that you will always support and accept your child in every way. Make it a habit to communicate empathy and acceptance from time to time.

- **Be the change you want to see**

  As parents we often have a lot of expectations from the child, but we forget that one needs to be the torchbearer for the change first. For every change that you would like to see in your child, become that first. For instance, we want our children to eat everything, but do we eat everything? We want our children to be assertive, but are we able to assert ourselves? Ask these questions before you set goals for the child and if you are successfully following through, guide your child to achieve the goal. This year try to be the change rather than just wanting to see the change.

The key to following through with resolutions is to keep them simple. Each time you feel like you are not able to stick to your resolve, instead of giving up just keep at it. Remember consistency is more important than perfection. So as you stretch your arms out to embrace another year, do so in the spirit of the immortal words of Benjamin Franklin, 'Resolve to perform what you ought; perform without fail what you resolve.'

4

Choosing the Right School

From the day the child is born, parents start preparing for the day that s/he will start going to school. Now children are enrolled into mother-and-toddler programmes at twelve months of age and graduate to playschools by eighteen months. By the time the child is twenty-four months old, parents start getting anxious about formal school admissions. Schools are no longer seen as centres of education but have assumed a much larger role in the lives of parents and children.

For most parents, the criterion of school selection is the 'name of the school' or its brand value. It is assumed that if the school is popular, it is good for the child's cognitive, social and emotional development. The brand value of the school promises access to the 'right social circles' and offers networking opportunities to parents as well as children from a future career perspective. This puts immense pressure on the child and parent to secure admission into a coveted school, and if things do not go as per plan, the parent feels distraught. What the parent fails to realize is that admission into a branded school does not necessarily translate into realizing the child's talents and potential or self-esteem.

While choosing schools it is important to have the broad goal to seek an institution that keeps the spark of curiosity alive, uncovers and nurtures the unique talents that the child possesses and equips him/her with the requisite social and life skills to become a capable human being.

The guideposts that can help in achieving this goal and finding the 'right fit' for your child's needs include:

- **Mode of schooling**

  Schooling is no longer limited to children attending traditional schools. Parents can opt for home-schooling or virtual schooling as alternatives to traditional schools. Traditional schools have a planned/structured curriculum, exposure to a variety of subjects, skilled teachers/instructors, access to sports and extracurricular activities, an opportunity to socialize with peers and may provide a platform to teach the child how to cope with constant competition and peer pressure.

Home-schooling may not be able to provide these requisites but offers more flexible schedules, encourages the child to gain knowledge and not to compete, is more focused on subjects of interest, facilitates parent–child bonding and may be devoid of bullying or harassment. Virtual schooling is emerging as an alternative mode of education globally and offers the opportunity to follow a structured curriculum through skilled teachers/instructors via a flexible schedule. Children are taught through integrated technology, which can be tailored to individual needs.

- **Logistics**

The first thing to consider is the teacher–student ratio. For younger children, it should ideally be one teacher for ten children.

The next thing to consider is whether you want your children to attend after-school academic, sports and co-curricular classes which help nurture the child's talents and interests. For a child to be able to enjoy these classes, the distance and commute time between the school and home should be minimal.

Each school has a range of after-school sports and co-curricular activities that can provide a suitable alternative to multiple after-school classes. Some schools rely more on technology as a teaching and learning tool as compared to others. This can prove a good fit for parents who feel that technology is vital for education and like to give their children tech devices from an early age. Parents who prefer traditional learning tools and are averse to exposing young children to screens can opt for schools that strike a balance between traditional teaching/ learning methods and technology.

The choice of transport to commute is an important factor to be considered. If you would like to opt for the school bus, it is important to ensure that all safety guidelines, such as verified drivers and experienced support staff, are in place. Some schools also provide a GPS and an in-bus camera for monitoring the children, which can help you keep track of the bus route and the child.

Fee structures are one of the most vital components of the decision-making process. While paying attention to the fee heads, it is important that you factor in the yearly increment and also consider the number of children you have. Along with this, add a 30 per cent additional overhead cost for miscellaneous items like school supplies or clothes for functions, birthday party expenses, etc. Once you have the figures worked out, you can choose the school which is the best financial fit for you.

- **School infrastructure**
The infrastructure of a school has a profound impact on the child's learning. Schools which have more natural light and are earthy and well ventilated facilitate learning as compared to those with minimal windows and heavily dependent on artificial lighting.

Special attention needs to be paid to the washrooms as small children should ideally have height-adjusted water closets and sinks for easy access to provide the child with a sense of independence in caring for him/herself. Clean and hygienic kitchens are equally important if the school has an in-house cafeteria and provides lunch. Schools which offer lunch are an asset as the child learns to eat everything and is taught how to serve him/herself and clean up after.

Choosing between an air-conditioned versus non-air-conditioned school is about parental preference. One may argue that since we have been accustomed to air conditioning in our cars and homes, it should also be available in school buses and classrooms. Another point of view may be that non-air-conditioned schools are healthier due to natural ventilation and can help the child learn to endure all types of situations. Air purifiers in schools are also a growing trend owing to the increase in dust allergies and pollution. For children with weak immune systems, air purifiers can be a boon. On the other hand, too much reliance on air purifiers may decrease immunity and be a bane in the long term.

School visits are a great way to assess logistics and infrastructure and can be arranged by contacting schools before the formal admission process begins. If the schools do not permit the same, parents can try to get in touch with parents of children enrolled in the school and ask for the requisite information.

- **Emphasis**
The core values of a school or the mission statement of the school says a lot about its approach. Syncing the school's values with parents' values is key to making the right choice. For some parents, academics are the sole focus in schools, while others may want a holistic development of the child

with a balance between academic, sports and co-curricular activities. Academically oriented schools are focused on performance and may be seen as a vehicle to prepare children for competitive exams later in life. The schools that follow a balanced approach are suited for children who may not be academically inclined and have other talents that can go unrecognized in an academically oriented school. Parents can consider the school's performance in the most recent board examinations (pass percentage of the school and highest marks obtained by children in different subjects), access to exchange programmes, participation in sports and co-curricular competitions and the record of university admissions to help them select the right school. Some schools have special wings for children with special needs or may believe in mainstreaming them and having a dedicated counsellor to help them. If your child has special needs then it is important to consider this aspect.

Schools usually have a parent–teacher association (PTA) which helps to bridge the gap between the school and parents. Having an active and responsive PTA body ensures that the school gives due regard to parents' views and concerns.

- **Staff**

  The staff's attitude, expertise and behaviour should be considered during the admission process. The first people you encounter at the gate are the security staff who are responsible for the security of the children and other staff within the premises. The best time to observe the security staff is when the school starts in the morning or when it ends. If the staff is not checking identity cards properly or allowing unknown persons to enter, then it should be seen as a cause of concern. The responsiveness of persons at the school reception is the next thing that parents should be mindful of. Having a list of questions handy for the school reception staff allows you to gauge how well the staff is trained to communicate and respond to parental concerns. Positive interaction and learning experiences with teachers are crucial for the overall development of the child. Since at the time of admission it may not be possible for parents to interact with the teaching staff, it is a good idea to speak to parents and children of the school that you are interested in applying for and finding reliable discussion forums that can tell you about teacher interactions and expertise. The support staff form an integral part of the school, especially for younger children as they actively help them with a lot of things such as using the washroom or during the snack/lunch break.

Make sure that the school holds regular sensitization programmes for their support staff and ensures that they follow standard hygiene practices. In addition, ensure that the school has a strict recruitment policy with a thorough background check and references.

• **Curriculum**

The curriculum is considered by some to be the backbone of schooling. The choice of board is a critical factor while considering admission. There are mainly four boards that are popular in Indian schools. These include the Central Board of Secondary Education (CBSE), Council for the Indian School Certificate Examination–Indian Certificate of Secondary Education/Indian School Certificate (CISCE–ICSE/ISC), International Baccalaureate (IB) and Cambridge Assessment International Education (Cambridge International). These differ broadly in terms of their focus and approach, subjects, criteria of assessment and the level of difficulty. Parents can choose the board that is aligned with their needs and beliefs.

The CBSE is followed in the majority of schools across India and is considered easier on the difficulty level and cheaper in terms of fee as compared to the others. It is geared towards rote learning and memorization, and is useful for those preparing for competitive medical and engineering entrance examinations.

The CISCE board is more complex than CBSE and is geared towards developing language skills with an emphasis on humanities and management streams. It is concept based and helps the child develop a well-rounded personality.

The IB board is geared towards developing analytical and logical reasoning as well as language skills. There is an emphasis on co-curricular activities and social work, which are essential for those who wish to pursue education abroad. The children are assessed the whole year round and emphasis is on internal assessments via assignments.

The Cambridge International board has international recognition and has a tough and demanding curriculum with a focus on expanding the child's knowledge base. It is useful for children who would like to pursue their education abroad. It has no fixed subject combinations and has a wide variety of subjects to choose from. Oral and problem-solving skills are given due importance along with written assignments.

While keeping in mind these pointers, it is important to follow your intuition or gut feeling. At times your child may not get admission in your preferred school owing to the selection criteria or some other factor unknown to you. Instead of feeling crushed, it is important to understand that it is not the end of the road for your child. You can always apply again or opt for a different school which may be better suited to your child's needs. Remember to hope for plan A to succeed but be prepared with plan B as well!

5

How to Make Reading
Interesting for Kids

We all know books give us wings of imagination and have the superpower to transport us anywhere and enlighten our minds with knowledge. Gone are the days when knowledge came solely from books. Today, children have a lot of resources at their disposal and online platforms with e-learning modules have become the main source of learning. While these mediums have their advantages, more than three hours of screen time puts children and adolescents at risk of developing 'computer vision syndrome', which includes symptoms like eye strain, headaches, blurred vision, dry eyes as well as neck and shoulder pain.

With the health costs of the screen being high, conventional sources of knowledge and entertainment such as books, comics, magazines, etc. offer a much healthier alternative for children.

Reading offers various benefits for children:

1. Reading to the child from an early age helps to strengthen the emotional bond between the parent and child and provides him/her a sense of security and comfort.

2. Becoming familiar with phonetic structures of words, word meanings and usage of words in sentences helps to develop a good vocabulary, language and comprehension skills.

3. Reading aids brain development by sharpening attention and concentration, memory and sequencing ability.

4. Reading material can be used to enhance divergent thinking or the ability to look at things differently and find solutions, which is an invaluable life skill.

5. Reading stories can help teach children social skills as well as facilitate emotional awareness and expression.

Despite innumerable benefits, making reading a part of the child's routine may be a struggle for some parents. Here are some ways in which you can make reading interesting and fun so that it becomes a way of life for your child:

1. **Start small and keep it simple**

   Each child has a different pace and interest when it comes to reading. Though it is recommended that the choice of book be age appropriate, a simple way is to pick books with more pictures and less words, and then move to more words and less pictures. Younger children are visual learners, so having pictorial content with words helps him/her associate those words with the images and recognize them more efficiently. Having a visual image of what you read also helps you to retain it longer in your brain. If your child has a learning disability like dyslexia, you can encourage him/her by starting with very simple books to read and gradually move to ones that require more effort to read and understand.

2. **Get creative**

   Props or art and craft is a great medium to engage young children. Children can be encouraged to draw pictures of words and then use them to create a story. Letters and word doodles can also be used as a tactile learning aid to familiarize children with the way a letter or words are written or printed. Once a book is read aloud, the child can be encouraged to draw what s/he liked about the book or can be asked to make drawings to show what happened when. This activity encourages the child to learn sequencing, which aids grammar, comprehension and narration. Finger and hand puppets can also be created or used to read a story to make it more engaging for the child. Reading books aloud animatedly is a great way to engage young children and also helps to teach them emotional expression. For children with a learning disability, having pets or their favourite toys with them while they read can help reduce anxiety and build confidence.

3. **Five-finger retell**

To sharpen reading comprehension, use the 'five-finger retell' every time you or the child reads a story. Every story has five elements – setting, characters, problems, events and solution. Use your hand or ask the child to hold out his/her hand to summarize the story using the five fingers. Start with the thumb, which represents the setting or the place(s) where the story unfolds. Then move to the index finger, which represents the characters or the people/animals in the story. The middle finger represents the problem or conflict that the characters experience. The ring finger represents the events or the things that happen in the story. The little finger represents the solution or the way the characters solve the problem and the end of the story. This way of summarizing the story also sets the foundation for later academic skills of recounting large amounts of information efficiently.

4. **Readers' theatre**

This involves getting the child, who can read independently, to read aloud to develop reading fluency and confidence. Set up a make-believe set or stage for the child and then assign him/her a part to read aloud. This is a great way to teach the child when to pause and use voice modulation and intonation. This activity is also used in teaching public speaking. It can help in developing communication and social skills as well. Apart from making reading fun and interesting, it can also become a family bonding activity by involving siblings, parents or even members of the extended family.

5. **Reward every milestone**

Whether it is recognizing pictures or letters or reading aloud words and sentences, make sure that you reward your child by verbally appreciating and encouraging him/her. For smaller children, you could also make a star or smiley face or put a sticker for reading. Small rewards like these motivate children to keep up with their reading habits. You could also put a reward system in place, wherein if s/he reads every day for a week and gets a star each day, s/he could exchange those for a small reward like a new book. In addition, parents can create attractive certificates, medals or trophies for the child when s/he is able to move from assisted to independent reading.

6. **Practise pre-reading skills**
Pre-reading skills help the child read. Engaging in activities which enhance these is a great way to teach and motivate the child to read. Some activities which help develop these skills include using phonetics – making the child aware of the sounds each letter makes and then combining these to form a word; syllabification – splitting a big word into smaller chunks and clapping after reading aloud every chunk; rhyming and word blast – finding rhyming words or asking the child to come up with as many words with particular letters can help boost vocabulary; and consonant–vowel–consonant (CVC), sight words and blends – encouraging the child to find and underline CVC words which use phonetic sounds (for instance, b-a-t uses consonants b and t with a vowel in the middle), sight words

which do not use phonetic sounds (for instance, he, the, etc.) and blends (for instance, combining the first two or last two letters to form a word like sn-o-w) can aid in word recognition and reading.

7. **Let your child choose**

Just like you take your child to a toy store and let him/her pick the one s/he likes, take children to libraries and bookstores and let them pick and choose a book. Instead of choosing books for your kids, allow them to feel invested in the process of selecting the book. You could choose one and let the child choose another. For the books that are purchased, the child can be encouraged to write his/her name on the front page and the date on which s/he got the book. The child can keep the book by his/her bedside till s/he moves on to the next book.

8. **Demonstrate the art of handling a book**

A step to making reading a personal experience is to teach the child how to read and care for the book. At times parents may not allow children to hold and read books due to the fear that s/he may tear or damage it. This only makes the child feel uncomfortable and s/he may avoid books altogether.

Instead of keeping the book from the child, allow him/her to hold the book when you are reading aloud. Demonstrate that the words in a sentence are read from left to right by using the pointer finger (index finger) and that after reading all the lines the page can be turned by lifting it from the top right corner. Make the child aware that just like we stay in a house, the book must be kept back in its house or the bookshelf after reading.

9. **Be a role model**

    Children learn from example and inculcating reading habits are no different. If you as a parent do not read books or are more interested in watching content online, you can't expect the child to be an avid reader. Make sure that you read on a daily basis before you expect the child to do so. As children become more independent in reading on their own, you can turn the bedtime ritual of reading out aloud into family reading time, where you can read your individual books.

10. **Book exchanges, book clubs and literary festivals**

    Children can be encouraged to exchange books with their friends to inculcate the habit of reading and sharing. Parents and children can initiate book clubs with their friends and classmates, where parents/children can read out stories or excerpts on rotation or discuss a book that they read recently. Signing up children for reading programmes or having access to libraries is a great way to teach them how to be environmentally conscious by reusing books and reducing the carbon footprint. Children's literature festivals offer an enriching experience by providing access to literary works from across the globe and through storytelling sessions by authors. Getting children to explore literature from different genres and languages adds diversity to their reading experience.

While introducing children to the written word and encouraging them to imbibe the reading habit, it is vital that you cultivate patience and stay consistent in reading a little bit every day. If you notice that the child is finding it difficult to read words and tends to get confused between letters, doesn't recognize rhyming patterns or has trouble in spelling words, and despite making a lot of effort is not able to make progress, then s/he may need to be evaluated by a mental health professional for learning disabilities and could benefit from early intervention. On the other hand, if your child shows a flair for reading, creative writing or storytelling, make sure to nurture it by signing up for workshops, sending writing samples to publishers and getting him/her to interact with authors.

6

10 Ways to Help Kids Ace Exams

The word 'exam' has a unique quality – it can create a sense of dread in the minds of most parents, the reason being the constant comparison and competition that starts from an early age. We aspire to be one up on the next person and want the same for our children too. Earlier, children would feel the pressure of giving exams in class ten and twelve but now even a class test translates into a 'do-or-die situation'. Such is the aura of examinations that parents start scheduling their lives around exam dates. As soon as the school calendar is released, instead of looking for holidays, parents scan it for exam dates. The next step is to ensure that the house becomes like a monastery during those periods – the cable connection is cut off, the phone is snatched and social life is off limits. The child is constantly told not to waste time and focus on finishing the syllabus. The fairy tale that 'marks will guarantee success in life' is told again and again. As the day of truth arrives, last-minute details are fed along with breakfast with the favourite parting words 'just do your best and don't worry'. After the exam is over, the paper is dissected question by question. Parents and tutors probe the child to know the minutest details and often let out exasperated sighs if a point or, God forbid, question was missed. In the whole drama of preparation to results, parents are often oblivious to how the child is emotionally coping with the strain of expectations. Unsuspectingly at times, this strain pushes children over the edge, leading either to an emotional breakdown or drastic steps like suicide.

As parents our goal should not be focused on pushing children to score a certain percentage, rather it should be on teaching them to effectively manage exam stress and perform to the best of their ability. Here are ten ways to help children ace their exams:

1. **Relaxation and visualization**

    A calm mind is better equipped to cope with stress and promotes clarity of thought. Make it a habit of doing simple breathing exercises with your child daily. For instance, you can do a set of ten deep breaths each – focusing first on the abdomen and then on the chest and the nose. Make sure that you do the exercises in a relaxed environment and not on a full stomach. After doing the relaxation exercise, ask your child to close his/her eyes to visualize the day of the exam. Tell him/her to visualize that the exam paper has questions which s/he is able to solve easily and emphasize that throughout the exam s/he is feeling calm and confident. Relaxation and visualization exercises help in training the mind to be calm and focused, thereby making the child feel more confident during the exam.

2. **Mental gymnastics**

The prefrontal cortex of the brain is the seat of attention, concentration, reasoning and problem-solving, all of which contribute to a sharp intellect. Stimulating this area by some simple mental exercises helps to improve attention, concentration and memory, which help in performing better in exams. Simple five- to ten-minute daily exercises like humming or chanting 'Aum' every morning, engaging in word/number puzzles, cancelling select letters or words in a paragraph or on a page can be done with children from an early age to train their brains to concentrate and retain information better and study more effectively. During exam days these exercises also serve as a healthy distraction from the stress, encourage quick thinking and foster a sense of mastery.

3. **Studying smart versus studying hard**

   Every exam paper has a pattern with certain topics carrying more weightage than others. Children often fall in the trap of trying to prepare the whole syllabus perfectly. With time constraints and a large amount of information to be retained, a better strategy is to review examination papers of the past five to ten years and focus first on preparing the topics which have more weightage and then proceeding to the ones with lower weightage. There may be some topics which are easy to grasp, while others may take more time and be difficult. Ask the child to prepare the tougher topics on days when s/he is more productive and has more time. The easier ones can be kept for days when s/he has lesser time or is not very focused or motivated. While detailed notes may be ideal, quick reference points for each topic are more beneficial to revise a lot of material in a short period of time.

4. **Study schedules**

Our body and mind respond well to consistent schedules. For instance, if you set the alarm and start waking up at a particular time every day, after a while you will automatically start waking up at that time without the alarm. Most children prefer to study late at night and sleep through the morning on holidays. What they don't realize is that the brain starts getting stimulated at night and becomes lethargic in the morning. Since most exams are conducted in the morning, it is important to ensure proper rest and sleep at night and stimulate the brain in the morning. While practising exam papers or preparing study material on holidays, try to sync it with the usual exam timings so that the brain is alert and trained to be the most active at that time. Even if your child prefers studying in the evening, make sure that s/he maintains the regular sleep–wake routine and doesn't study beyond 9 p.m.

5. **Engage all the senses**

Children often make the mistake of just learning material by reading and cramming. While this method may work for people with a photographic memory, it doesn't help in retaining information for long periods. While studying, it is important to ensure that all senses are involved in the learning process. Teachers, for instance, are able to reproduce a lot of information without referring to the books in class. This is because they read the material, write it, speak it aloud, hear it and put it in context with examples. Studying in a holistic manner and in a way like one would teach the same to another is the best way to learn. To ensure longer retention, ask the child to visualize the concept and teach it to an imaginary student or even to the family pet. In addition, have him/her revise the material within twenty-four hours of studying the topic.

6. **Short breaks**

The average attention span of children varies according to age – a three- to six-year-old can pay attention for six to twenty minutes, a seven- to ten-year-old for eighteen to thirty minutes and an eleven- to sixteen-year-old for thirty to fifty minutes. To study better, it is important to keep the average attention span in mind and take short breaks. For instance, an average child studying in class four can study well at a stretch for thirty minutes and then needs a five- to ten-minute break to refocus. Taking short and frequent breaks helps children study for a longer duration with minimal fatigue. However, it is important to bear in mind that the breaks should be uneventful like drinking water or just moving around a bit rather than watching television. Uneventful breaks help in getting back on track with ease and not procrastinate. In addition to short breaks between study periods, it is important that parents do not block all sources of entertainment for the child. Instead of having the child focus more on studies, it may have the opposite effect of him/her thinking more about the distractions. Having the child engage in a pleasurable activity every day within the healthy limit of an hour helps to recharge the mind and body.

7. **Be aware of the child's ability**
Every child has a different ability, be it academic or co-curricular. Even in academics, some children perform well in certain subjects and not in others. When setting goals about marks and performance in examinations, keep his/her ability in mind and set targets accordingly. For instance, if your child usually scores 70 per cent in his/her exams, setting a goal of 95 per cent may be unreasonable and may cause undue stress or pressure. A goal of 75 to 80 per cent may be more reasonable and attainable. Setting a reasonable goal doesn't mean putting in

less effort. The child should be encouraged to put in his/her best but not pressurize him/herself about getting a very high percentage.

8. **Make exams a habit**
The concept of joining test series is a popular practice among engineering and medical aspirants. Getting your child to practise giving tests/exams regularly is a great way to reduce exam anxiety and improve time management. Since most children prefer to learn by reading and cramming and are not in the habit of writing, they struggle to complete exam papers. Regular tests help in overcoming this issue and ensure that the child is able to complete the paper and revise it before submission. In addition, this exercise helps the child study on a consistent basis and helps him/her become aware of problem areas which need to be addressed and practised more.

9. **External help**
Just like adults, some children take initiative and are self-motivated while others need a constant push or external motivation. Self-motivated children are able to study on their own and, if need be, thrive in a group tuition setting. Children who are

more reserved and have difficulty with grasping academic concepts usually benefit from one-to-one tuition. Parents at times either feel guilty about starting tuitions for children or go overboard by relying solely on tuitions from preschool for all subjects. While seeking external help is a good idea to keep the child academically engaged, it should not become the sole way of learning. Striking a balance by motivating the child to engage in self-study and, if needed, taking additional help makes them more confident and self-sufficient.

10. Support unconditionally

As parents, we engage in the barter system with our children from an early age. 'Get 90 per cent and I will get you whatever you want' is a dialogue we hear in various forms at different points of time. Barter has become an inherent part of our lives, often becoming a bane rather than a boon. The child at times may feel pressured to be a certain way or perform to a standard to gain parental appreciation and love. If s/he fails more than once, it may foster poor self-esteem or feelings of not being good enough. We as parents should love our children unconditionally, but somewhere along the path we start loving them conditionally. It is important to communicate to our children on a regular basis that it is okay to fail at times or not meet targets, and that as parents we will always accept and love them. Nagging children to study is never an effective way to motivate them. Restrict the reminders to study to just once or twice and communicate to the child that ultimately s/he is responsible for preparing well for the exam and that you trust him/her to do the right thing. Instead of quizzing children about how the exam went, give them time to come and talk about it.

Despite best efforts, at times children may not do well. Instead of feeling disheartened, you can use these five strategies to make the child feel better:

1. **Let the child express his/her frustration:** Be empathetic instead of sympathetic. If s/he feels frustrated about not performing well, tell the child that even though you may not be able to feel the same level of frustration that s/he is going through, you are there to support him/her and love him/her. Let the child cry and don't shy away from giving a hug.

2. **Reduce anxiety by distraction:** When a child is very disturbed, offering rational advice doesn't work. Try

to distract the child by engaging in an activity that takes his/her mind off the result and helps him/her calm down.

3. **Plan the next steps:** Once the child is in a better frame of mind, sit with him/her and discuss what s/he feels could have been done differently. Help the child embrace the learning from the experience and come up with a plan to do better next time.

4. **Normalize failures:** Instead of making a failure look like the end of the world, help the child understand that it is just an obstacle which can be overcome. Use examples from your life where you may have failed or performed poorly to make it relatable.

5. **Consult a professional:** If the child is inconsolable, highly anxious or has mentioned harming him/herself in any way, please consult a mental health professional.

At the end of the day, exams are not a thing to be feared but a challenge that needs to be embraced from time to time!

7

Parenting in the Age of Tech

'Select, click and go!' is the new mantra for millennials. Wherever you go, everyone is hooked to their phones. With technology enmeshed in every aspect of one's life, parenting in the millennial age is no different. In today's age, parents-to-be install apps that intimate them about intimacy schedules, and when those magical lines appear on the pregnancy test kit, they click away on the subscribe buttons of blogs, support groups and the works. As the child arrives, feeding schedules are eased by feeding time browsing (FTB). The young child slowly becomes aware of the enchanting colours and sounds emanating from a little magic box. Parents and grandparents boast to their friends and family about the toddler being more adept than them at unlocking features on the smartphone, till one day a random aunty comments that the screen is not good for the child! The show-off strategy suddenly changes to 'we don't show any screen to our child . . .'

The tug of war between technology being a boon or a bane is evident at every stage of parenting. Most often parents feel forced to pick sides – including technology in or excluding it from their lives. The answer to the tech riddle is not a simple one. With technology being such an integral part of our lives, we cannot avoid it. Centuries ago, the Buddha propagated the 'middle path' or the path of moderation between indulgence and self-mortification. The same philosophy can be applied to parenting in the age of technology. The goal of parenting in the age of technology is to find the middle path between the 'Fear of Missing Out' (FOMO) and 'Over the Top' (OTT).

How much is too much?
The most debated topic related to technology among parents is screen. Screen encompasses all types of visual media (TV, computers, tablets, phones). There is a constant dilemma among parents regarding how much screen a child should watch. To solve this riddle, parents first need to ask themselves, 'how much time do I devote to the screen?' This is because children imitate

their parents and if parents are constantly hooked to their phones and gadgets, children follow suit.

Minimize the use of technology

The first step is to minimize the use of technology when you are spending time with your children. This will help you to serve as a positive role model and also give undivided attention to your children. The next step is to establish boundaries regarding how much screen time is acceptable. To determine the amount of screen time a child should be allowed, it is vital to understand the difference between active screen time and passive screen time. Active screen time is when you are actively engaged in watching the content. For instance, there are certain educational cartoons on TV, which engage the child by asking questions and stimulating their minds. Passive screen time on the other hand is just mindlessly watching videos on TV or the internet, which do nothing to stimulate the mind. According to health guidelines published by the World Health Organization (WHO), passive screen time should be limited to one hour for children between two and five years of age, with a parent co-watching to monitor the content. For older children, parents can limit the passive screen time to two hours and decide the active screen time on requirement basis, for instance, when the child has to do a school project which needs access to the internet and videos.

Cross-check online information

Parents of young children often grapple with numerous challenges in caring for their young ones. For every sneeze and cry, they turn to the internet and WhatsApp groups. Just the other day, on one of the parent WhatsApp groups that I am a part of, there was a heated exchange about which medicines to give sick kids for stomach ache, mouth ulcers, etc. While I was skimming through the responses, I wondered why this discussion was even taking place. Why is a visit to the doctor being excluded from the equation? Is it because 'rationality' has been traded for a 'social life'? Unfortunately, this tendency of turning to the internet and social media for everything and anything is a challenge posed at every age of a child's development. To strike a balance, it is important for parents to first understand that information needs to be 'vetted' and that they should use 'discrimination' before accepting things blindly. The easiest way to gain access to the 'right information' is by accessing authentic sources – pages of national and international organizations specializing in the field of interest (Wikipedia is unfortunately not an authentic source!). By empowering oneself with authentic knowledge, unnecessary panic is avoided and decision-making is facilitated.

Manage screen content

It is also important to consider screen content or what the child is accessing on the screen. While encouraging children to keep abreast with the latest developments in the tech space, it is important to be aware of the dangers that come up from time to time, particularly the ones that target children like the recent Blue Whale Challenge, which assigned a series of tasks to the players over a fifty-day period. Some of these tasks encouraged self-harm and the final task was to die by suicide. With uncensored content being freely available and accessible on the internet, it is important for parents to educate themselves about the features regarding content access and privacy settings on social media and web-based applications. For young children, who are impressionable, it is extremely vital for parents to choose the programmes. Many a time parents hand over the tablet/phone and ask the help to supervise. The child keeps swiping away, particularly on YouTube, and keeps viewing anything and everything that is clicked. If you can't watch along with the child, ensure that you are able to alter settings and put filters to ensure that certain content is restricted from view.

Ensure physical activity

Be sure to ensure that the child engages in physical activity every day to balance out the time spent on the screen. For instance, every hour spent on passive screen time should be balanced with an hour of activity. If you are a parent who doesn't have support and need the electronic babysitter to help you out with your infant and toddler, trade the screen for interactive toys. For instance, instead of letting the child use the phone as a toy, use other battery-operated toys with sounds and lights, or simply turn on rhymes or soothing music on the phone and keep it at a distance. If that doesn't work well at times and you do give in to letting your child watch the screen, don't feel guilty. Just keep trying various alternatives.

Tech-free time

Encourage yourself and your children to spend some time during the day away from technology. You can introduce the concept of tech-free time, when all family members are barred from using any form of technology or screens. Implementing any new routine takes time, so be patient and consistent and don't discontinue just because of a slip. Think of tech-free activities before implementing this concept to ease the transition. Also, teach your children from an early age to draw their self-esteem from their abilities and not from people's perceptions or comments. Parents keep sharing their own pictures obsessively to garner attention in the form of likes/comments to boost their self-image and self-esteem. The child is a spectator to all this and starts emulating the same behaviour and starts linking the adulation on social media to validation for self-esteem. While the temptation to lead a utopian life on social media may be difficult to resist, it is important to live in the moment than through the lens or on the web.

Talk to your child

Maintaining open communication is a crucial aspect in parenting and is the most effective way to monitor your child's tech habits. Instead of snooping or checking their phones or screens behind their back, talk to them about your fears and about objectionable content on the web. Often parents don't want to talk about porn or cyberbullying or mindless social media challenges. They feel that it may increase the child's curiosity and make him/her want to access it, or at times they delude themselves that it can never happen with their child. What they don't realize is that if they talk about things in a mature way, the child may become more aware of the dangers and hence not fall prey to such ills easily. In case your child wants to talk about any kind of objectionable content, have an open discussion without condemning or judging.

While keeping the communication channels open, it is important to watch out for certain signs which may suggest that your child needs help. These include:

1. Spending a lot of time on social media or gaming sites, so much so that s/he prefers the screen rather than spending time with friends.
2. The child's appetite and sleep cycles have changed and s/he is not caring for her/himself as a result of the time spent on the screen.
3. The child has reduced his/her communication with family members or close friends and has become secretive.
4. There is a marked change in the child's academic performance, which can be attributed to more time spent on the screen than on studies.
5. The child has become very irritable, aggressive, anxious, etc. as a result of spending a lot of time on the screen and gets abusive if screen access is blocked.

If you observe and feel that your child is exhibiting any such signs, talk to your child and try to resolve the issue. Communicate your concerns with compassion and not judgement. Recognize that children are allowed to make mistakes, and with proper guidance they can do wonders. In case you as a parent feel overwhelmed and are not able to achieve a breakthrough with the child, do not shy away from consulting a mental health professional. Everyone needs a little help once in a while, no matter how accomplished and sorted they may be.

Technology can empower or devour, but you can ensure that your child has a choice and a voice!

8

7 Ways to Manage Kids While Working from Home

The recent health crisis of coronavirus has introduced a wave of challenges in our lives such as self-isolation, physical distancing, managing the house without helpers and working from home with children around. Rather than focusing on these changes as deterrents, perceive them as vital life lessons which will equip you and your children with novel life skills and coping methods.

Contrary to modern belief, the concept of working from home is not new. Women and mothers have been doing it for ages. With the advent of modern civilization and amenities, we became more conditioned to regard the concept of work as something which is outside our homes. Similarly, managing children also became a task delegated to various persons and institutions. Hence, the present crisis forces us to slow down and reflect on how we can make our lives less complicated and more efficient. If we keep an open mind and adopt a seeker's attitude, we can learn to adapt to any crisis and manage various aspects of our life including work and children effectively.

Drawing from age-old wisdom and modern psychological principles, here are seven useful tips which can help you manage your kids efficiently while you work from home.

1. **Expect less and accept more**

   The first and the most important thing is to understand that when you are working from home, you can't have the same schedule and routine that you have in an office set-up. You will have doorbells, children fighting and other disruptions from time to time. Since most of these cannot be controlled, expect that you will be able to achieve 40 to 60 per cent of what you do on a typical office workday. If you keep your expectations reasonable and low, you will feel better when you are able to get more done. Accept disruptions and distractions of all kinds as part of the process and instead of getting irritated or overwhelmed, work at resolving the issues that crop up and then get back to work. For instance, if your children start a fight, get up and resolve the fight rather than shouting at them or feeling helpless.

2. **Identify productive and non-productive time slots**
    There are certain time slots in a day when you are more productive or can put in more effort, for instance, when the children are sleeping, watching the screen or are engaged in an activity – be it studying or playing on their own. Plan your workday in a way that you can do more pressing or important work during these times. Children are more demanding at certain time intervals, for instance, during mealtimes or in the later part of the day when they are tired. Observe your child's pattern and once you know the time slots when s/he is demanding or cranky, keep your work light and flexible so that you can attend to your kid/s.

3. **Work as a team**
    Delegate responsibilities to family members. Parents and family members can take turns in engaging the kid/s so that everyone can get their work done, get some downtime and also enjoy time with each other. If there is an important work call/meeting or you need to take two to four hours to finish some

urgent work, inform your spouse/family members in advance to take over and manage the children. Make sure to be appreciative every time a family member or your spouse helps. This motivates everyone to work together and doesn't lead to people being taken for granted and feeling underappreciated.

4. **Strike a balance while planning activities**

   Nobody likes monotony, especially children. While planning children's daily activities, divide into four categories – daily chores, leisure, exercise and learning. Make a list of activities in each category. Suggestions for the same can be solicited from the children. Involving children in planning activities is a great way to make them feel invested in the process. At the start of every day, get the child to choose one activity from each category. You can also make a game and have the child pick chits from a bowl for each category. To motivate younger children to help in daily chores, you can make attractive superhero badges for them like 'Dust Buster', 'Mom's Helper', etc. Daily chores instil a sense of responsibility in children and make them understand the concept of work from an early age.

5. Incentivize productivity

To get your children to cooperate and help you make the most of your day, make sure you reward them. You can use a simple reward system like stars for younger children or tokens for elder ones for completing the activities planned for the day. These stars or tokens can be exchanged for special treats like extra minutes of screen time or a phone call with a friend, etc. This will ensure that they are gainfully occupied for longer periods of time and give you space to finish your work. For every activity done well or when they have cooperated with you, praise their efforts. A word of praise goes a long way and helps to motivate children to follow through with their routine activities with a smile.

6. Have physical and emotional outlets in place

It has been observed in many social experiments and popular shows that when you have people spending a lot of time in a confined space, they keep getting into conflicts and meltdowns become a usual feature. The same holds true when you and your children are at home for long periods. Having physical outlets in the form of certain simple indoor exercise routines or engaging in some breathing exercises is useful to expend internal frustrations and energize your mind and body with positivity. In a similar way, there may be times when family members or children get on each other's nerves. On such occasions it is important to have constructive distractions like venting to a friend or listening to some good music. Make sure that you do not overindulge in distractions as that may lead to a domino effect of not getting work done at all.

7. **Keep communication channels open and underscore accessibility**
This is vital to make a success of any situation. Communicate your expectations of how you have planned your workday with your family members so that everyone can cooperate with each other. Tell your children that there will be certain times in the day when you may be busy with work or on a call but that they can approach you in case they have a problem. Children older than six years are usually able to understand the concept of their parents taking time to attend to work and cooperate if they are asked to keep themselves engaged while you attend to something important. Younger children may keep coming up to you for something or the other from time to time, but if you patiently attend to them and distract them, they are more likely to

let you do your work as compared to when you keep dismissing them or getting irritated with them.

Be assertive while handling kids – tell them what they need to do without shouting or getting exasperated. If they disobey you, you can impose timeouts or withdrawal of certain privileges. Even though you may not be going to office or the child may not be attending school, keep the sleep–wake cycle the same as regular days. It helps in maintaining a certain level of routine and control over the day. While you balance working from home and managing kids, remember to go through the day one task at a time. Pigeonholing activities helps in staying focused on the task at hand and not getting overwhelmed. Last but not the least, take ten minutes every day to let your hair down and make the most of the limited moments of solitude!

9

Why Do Kids Lie?

The biggest lie we tell our children is 'you should never lie and never hide anything from me', but as parents we tend to bend the truth ourselves. We expect our children to become beacons of morality, while we err all the time. We are quick to reprimand and punish, but rarely do we reflect on the concept of lying and the reasons behind it.

The concept of lying is not the same for every age. Just the other day I noticed a new drawing on the wall and my three-year-old holding a crayon in her hand. As I reached for the wonder wipe, I asked her, 'Did you do this?' As expected, pat came the response, 'No.' Going by the usual manual of morality, I should have snatched the crayon and reprimanded her for lying to me, but my training in psychology came to my rescue.

Children under the ages of four to five do not really

know the difference between telling the truth and lying. The lies toddlers usually tell are those which ensure that the parent will not get upset with them. They assume that everyone thinks about things in the same way and that the parent will believe whatever they say. As children grow up and their brains mature, they are able to understand that people may have different ideas and thoughts. They also understand that the concept of right and wrong may not be the same for everyone. So if my five-year-old scribbled on the wall and was holding the crayon, he would tell me that the drawing was made by my three-year-old and that he had taken the crayon from her. The lie would be more believable as he understands that I would not be convinced until I am shown a different scenario.

For children, the ability to lie is like a developmental milestone that shows their minds can creatively conjure up alternative realities, and that they can manipulate them. It is a sign that their brains are maturing and they are able to think differently. Apart from cognitive development, lying behaviour also offers insights into social development. Children with good social skills are more convincing when they lie as compared to those with poor social skills.

If lying serves as an indicator for cognitive and social development, why is it such a problem?

Children usually lie with either an intention to help/not harm someone (prosocial lying) or to benefit themselves at the expense of others (antisocial lying). The first type constitutes harmless white lies, such as pretending to like a gift that was given by a close friend. The second type, which is taken as the literal definition of lying, should be discouraged actively from a young age. Apart from considering the type of lies told, it is important to pay attention to the pattern of lying as well. If the child or adolescent resorts to persistent lying, it should be seen as a red flag. Some useful tips to curb lying in children include:

- **Walk the talk**
  Children of all ages observe the way their parents deal with situations and people. We are great at giving sermons to our children about the difference between right and wrong and expect them to be the flagbearers of truth, but seldom do we reflect on how much we practise what we preach. Not resorting to lies is a utopian concept. Instead of asking children never to lie, talk to them about trying to be truthful as much as possible. It is important to tell them that at times you also lie and that it is not a sin, but telling lies which harm people or unjustly benefit us need to be avoided. Parents need to reflect on their

75

patterns from time to time and try to be positive role models.

- **Stories and audiovisual media**
  If you go back to your childhood, you will surely remember your parents telling you the story of Pinocchio – the puppet whose nose grew when he lied. Storybooks with beautiful illustrations or short animated videos are a great way to introduce moral concepts to young children. Parents can watch short films on YouTube or TED Talks on concepts like honesty and lying with their teenagers and young adults. This can be followed by a light discussion or dinner table conversation around it. Such activities increase awareness about the consequences of lying and help children and teens understand that they can choose the path of truth or lies.

- **Art**
  Art is a great way of communicating with children as it helps to channelize emotions in an unthreatening manner. Children feel more comfortable opening up about any issue or problem when engaged in art-based activities as compared to being directly confronted by parents or adults. They are also less likely to lie if asked about certain things while

they are drawing or painting. In addition, toddlers and preschoolers can be engaged in craft activities around stories like Pinocchio to help them associate lying with negative consequences.

- **Problem-solving activities**

  These are great to get teenagers to think about the consequences of their actions. For instance, provide a scenario of a teen who performs poorly in examinations and lies about his grades. Discuss the possible consequences of the teen's actions and offer suggestions for helping the teen tell the truth. Another activity is using 'decision-balancing' or listing the pros and cons of lying and being honest. This will help the teen think about consequences and pick honesty over lies.

- **Truth checks**

  Children often lie impulsively when they are confronted or cornered by parents or adults. Truth checks are a simple way of giving a child time to think before responding and thereby not falling into the trap of lying. For instance, a teacher may complain that the child has not been eating the meal served at school. Instead of confronting the child, you can approach her/him by asking if s/he would like to tell you something about the meal served at school. If the child responds in the negative, you can tell her/him that you will be back in ten minutes and ask the question again just in case s/he wants to give a different answer. Mention that it's a truth check and that s/he would not be punished in any way.

- **Timeout and loss of privileges**
Pairing a behaviour with a negative consequence helps to weaken it over time. For instance, every time the child lies about issues like not completing homework or hitting another child, parents can give him/her a timeout by asking the child to face a wall or stay in a corner for a certain period of time to make him/her realize that mistake. Teenagers can be deprived of certain privileges like their phones or attending their friends' parties for a certain period of time to discourage them from lying.

- **Reward honesty**
Each time your child or teen owns up to a mistake and comes clean about a lie s/he may have told you, praise her/him for it. While it is easy to find faults, it is more important to reinforce positive actions so that the child learns to draw attention

from engaging in prosocial behaviours than from concealing negative ones.

- **Communication and acceptance**
  This is the key to solving any issue with your child. Children usually lie to parents to avoid disapproval or punishment. Every child wants approval, be it from parents, peers or teachers. If a child is assured that s/he will be accepted regardless of her/his faults and mistakes, s/he feels secure enough to speak the truth. Most of us are programmed to immediately reprimand negative behaviour, including lying. Instead of choosing the autopilot reprimand mode, try to instil a sense of security in your child from an early age. Tell her/him that you will accept her/him with love for any mistake or failing. Reinforce that though you would like them to choose virtue over vice, it is not necessary for them to be embodiments of virtue.

- **Professional guidance**
  Lying coupled with other antisocial behaviours like stealing, bunking school, getting into arguments and fights or use of alcohol, tobacco and drugs should be urgently addressed by consulting a mental health professional. Persistent lying in childhood coupled

with antisocial behaviours may be a symptom of conduct disorder, which may later turn into a personality disorder. Timely intervention in the form of counselling from trained mental health professionals can help parents and the child cope effectively and de-escalate the crisis.

Remember that if we as adults cannot always speak the truth, we should not judge our children for uttering a lie.

10

7 Ways to Discipline Kids

There are days in every parent's life when it gets overwhelming to handle the kid/s. It starts with a tantrum and before you know it, there is an urge to either shout or even hit the child. The aftermath is worse – you start guilt-tripping yourself.

Disciplining a child is not about punishing him/her but about teaching the importance of following certain rules and respecting boundaries. Each parent has a different style of parenting and it is this style or way of teaching the child how to behave that sets the tone for the way s/he behaves in a social situation or crisis.

Parenting styles usually fall into four main types. The first parenting style is 'authoritative' or 'supportive', where parents support their child and set clear rules about what is acceptable and what is not. The second parenting style is 'authoritarian', in which parents use punishment and anger to get children to follow certain rules that are non-negotiable. The third parenting style is 'permissive' or 'indulgent', in which parents go to any extent to make their child happy and do not believe in setting restrictions or rules. The fourth parenting style is 'neglectful', where parents are self-absorbed and not bothered about what is happening in their child's life. Most parents tend to follow a parenting style that is an amalgamation of these four depending on the situation they are in. At times we may feel the necessity to shout at the child or even raise a hand if s/he is misbehaving, and at other times we may buy them an expensive toy or gadget when we aren't able to spend much time with them. Even though we are tempted to switch between parenting styles as the situation demands, it is important that we use an authoritarian parenting approach as often as we can because children who are raised with this approach are more likely to be self-reliant, cooperative, achievement oriented and happy.

The seven ways to adopt an authoritative or supportive approach to parenting and disciplining a child are:

1. Be a role model

We have all heard the saying that the apple doesn't fall far from the tree. The same goes for disciplining your child. If you as a parent are not organized or disciplined, no matter how many sermons you preach to your child, s/he is not likely to be disciplined. If you are impatient and resort to shouting when stressed, you cannot expect your child to stay calm when his/her demands are not met. Discipline yourself first and lead by example. Each family member can be encouraged to choose one aspect of their behaviour they wish to improve and work towards it. In this way, you can inculcate an attitude of self-improvement, which is essential for leading a disciplined life.

2. **Set clear rules**

As parents, it is important to clearly outline what is acceptable and what is not. You can put up a chart with a set of family rules. For young children you can use pictures, while older children can write down the rules. Having a discussion with the children about what the rules should include is a great way of instilling a sense of ownership and responsibility. This activity also teaches negotiation, which is a vital life skill. Make sure that you start small with three to five rules and then edit or add more when the family is consistently following the rules. Keep in mind that the rules should not be unrealistic. For instance, 'never feeling angry' is not possible.

3. **Reward prosocial behaviour**

Children have a tendency to repeat behaviours that get parental attention. Their subconscious mind doesn't specifically distinguish between good and bad attention, and hence we find them repeating negative behaviours like temper tantrums again and again. To encourage a child to engage in prosocial and positive behaviour, it is important to reward the child. For young children, you can do so by maintaining an activity chart and giving a star each time s/he accomplishes a task. Once the child has earned stars for an activity every day in the week, s/he can exchange them for a small tangible reward. For older children, they can be given certain privileges for positive behaviour, for instance, if the child is consistently studying for an hour a day, s/he can be given an extra hour of television or internet access over the weekend. Along with tangible rewards or privileges, it is important for parents to praise and encourage the child each time s/he engages in desired behaviours. Reinforcing positive behaviours will ensure that the child keeps engaging in them.

4. **Discourage negative behaviour**

Parents should follow a zero-tolerance policy when it comes to the child engaging in any kind of negative behaviour. Each time your child says or does something which is disrespectful or wrong, s/he should be verbally reprimanded in a firm tone instead of being shouted or yelled at. For younger children, you need to kneel down to the child's eye level while telling him/her that a behaviour is unacceptable. Instead of raising your hand, use timeout as a means of discouraging negative behaviour. Assign a corner in the house that is not used for recreation as the timeout corner. Whenever the child misbehaves, put him/her in that corner for an amount of time which equals the child's age in minutes (for instance, a four-year-old is put on a timeout for four minutes). After the timeout period is over, explain to the child why s/he was given a timeout and ask for an apology. Once the child apologizes, hug the child and release him/her from the corner. In case the child refuses to apologize or throws a tantrum, keep him/her on timeout again for the same period. For older children, taking away a privilege for a week can be used as a strategy to discourage unacceptable behaviour, such as cutting off the television or internet time or taking away the phone, etc. Timeouts or withdrawing privileges gets the child to think about his/her actions and discourages him/her to engage in problematic behaviour.

5. **Explore healthier alternatives**

   The best way to eliminate unhealthy patterns of behaviour is to replace them with healthier alternatives. This can be achieved by, first, teaching children how to discriminate between positive and negative behaviour, and second, encouraging them to try out alternative positive ways of behaving. Make the child aware of the problematic behaviour and then discuss how s/he can change that behaviour. For instance, if your child throws things in anger, s/he can be taught anger management skills like venting the anger by punching a pillow or distracting him/herself. Maintaining open communication with children ensures that they understand there is a difference between reacting and responding to situations. Negative behaviour patterns are usually formed because children are reacting impulsively rather than thinking about the consequences. If they are encouraged to be more mindful about how they respond to situations, the likelihood of them falling prey to indiscipline is greatly reduced.

6. **Routines and responsibilities**

   Having your child follow a routine is essential to inculcate discipline. Regular routines ensure that the child is involved in constructive tasks throughout the day and doesn't have the time to engage in idle thoughts or deeds. Including a daily responsibility or chore is equally important, as learning to be responsible is the precursor to leading a disciplined life. Daily chores or responsibilities teach accountability and rising above likes, dislikes and whims. It also teaches the child to obey authority and follow instruction. Routines do not have to be rigid and can be a healthy mix of certain activities you expect your child to perform and an activity the child would like to engage in. For instance, you may set aside time for study as well as leisure on a daily basis.

7. **Be consistent**

A common sight in malls and at the marketplace is a child throwing a tantrum and asking the parent for a toy or a treat. The parent starts by refusing but when the tantrum intensifies and passers-by start staring, the parent, out of embarrassment and exasperation, yields to the demands. The same parent at home does not give in to tantrums but wonders why the child doesn't stop throwing tantrums altogether. The reason is simple – inconsistent disciplining. You cannot enforce discipline in one situation and not follow through in another. To discipline your child, you need to be consistent – whether it is routines, appreciating prosocial behaviour or reprimanding negative behaviour. The rule of thumb is that a behaviour needs to be consistently followed for at least twenty-one days for it to become a part of the person's demeanour.

As you discipline your child, remember that raising the perfect child is a utopian concept. It is important that your child's life isn't reduced to an assembly line. Accept that children will make mistakes, rebel and be undisciplined from time to time. As mentioned earlier, a parent's duty is to emulate the potter who beats the clay into shape but also supports it from within to make it beautiful. Despite your best efforts, if your child continues to misbehave and indulges in repeated lying, hitting, running away from school or home, damaging public property, harming animals or getting into trouble with the law, you should consult a mental health professional.

11

5 Ways to Stop Bullying

Contrary to what most people think, academics is not the only stress our children face today. There is another stress that lurks in the real and virtual lives of children and adolescents. 'Bullying' or using physical/emotional power to control or harm another often goes unnoticed as children and adolescents tend to suffer it in silence till breaking point.

Traditionally, bullying was face to face and restricted to school settings, where a child or a group of children would tease or trouble others. However, with the advent of technology and social media, this has transformed into an ugly version of cyberbullying. Cyberbullying involves sending, posting or sharing mean or false information about another. It can take place via electronic means through SMS, apps, social media, gaming forums or email.

There are mainly seven types of cyberbullying:

1. The first is 'flaming' and involves fighting online.
2. The second is 'harassment' and includes sending repeated offensive messages to a person.
3. The third is 'outing or trickery' and involves discovering personal information about a person and then sharing it without the person's consent.
4. The fourth constitutes 'exclusion' or blocking a person from friend lists or electronic communication.
5. 'Impersonation' is the fifth type of cyberbullying and involves pretending to be someone else and communicating negatively or inappropriately with others via electronic means.
6. The sixth type constitutes 'cyberstalking' or using electronic communication to stalk a person by sending repeated threatening messages.
7. The last type of cyberbulling is 'sexting', which involves sending naked or inappropriate photos without consent.

Whatever the form of bullying, it has far-reaching physical and psychological consequences that may range from somatic complaints such as headaches or stomach ache, absenteeism from school, poor academic performance, low self-esteem, anxiety, depressive symptoms and at times self-harm or suicide. These can be prevented if we pay attention to the warning signs or red flags.

The common warning signs that your child is being bullied are:

1. Unexplained complaints of frequent headaches, stomach ache or feeling unwell.
2. Lack of interest in activities which s/he enjoyed earlier.
3. Absenteeism or making excuses not to go to school or extracurricular classes.
4. Refusal to socialize with others or feeling isolated/lonely.
5. Trouble sleeping or experiencing frequent nightmares.
6. Unexplained injuries/bruises or loss/damaged clothing or belongings.
7. Threats of self-harm.
8. Complaints of children being mean, troubling him/her or making fun of him/her.

As parents, we may not be able to control all the situations that our children are exposed to, but we can ensure that they are well equipped with the knowledge and skills to stand up to bullying.

Here are five ways to prevent bullying and help your child stand up against it:

1. **Talk about it**

    The first step to counter bullying is to make your child aware of what bullying entails. Instead of talking about it only when the child faces such a situation, it is better to make children aware of it from an early age. With young children you can use drawings and stories to make the child understand how bullying takes place as well as what acts constitute bullying. With older children, short films or discussions can prove to be useful tools to explain the concept of bullying. When children start using technology, particularly social media, they should be made aware that while social media is a great way to connect with others, it is important to screen the people who have access to your posts or profile. Parents need to educate themselves about cybersecurity measures, which can be taught to children and teens, to ensure that in case of a situation of cyberbullying, they can take steps to curb it. Apart from educating children about bullying, it is also vital to make them aware that being a bystander enables bullying and that one should not encourage it by either being a silent witness or being party to it by enjoying someone else being heckled or teased. Encouraging children and teens to share their thoughts and feelings facilitates timely reporting of any uncomfortable incidents and fosters a sense of safety.

If your child reports an instance of being teased or children being mean to him/her, do not dismiss it as 'it's not a big deal' or 'handle your own problems and don't complain to me'. Instead, hear the child out and discuss how best the issue can be resolved and, if need be, personally intervene in the matter so that it doesn't happen again.

2. Establish boundaries

At a time when people publicly share every living moment on social media, it is vital to explain the concept of privacy and personal space from an early age. You can do this by engaging your child in a simple activity called 'the circle of closeness'. Start by making a circle in the middle of the page and label it as the 'inner circle'. This circle represents the people closest to us – family and friends whom we trust and with whom it is safe to share personal information. Make a second circle around the first one and label it as 'acquaintances'. This includes people you know and may interact with on a daily basis – teachers, household staff, neighbours, etc. These are people with whom you share lesser information than your inner circle – mostly on a need-to-know basis. Make a third circle around the second one and label it the 'outermost circle'. This represents strangers and people you meet once in a while. With this circle you do not share any personal information till you are sure that they can be trusted. Now ask your child to put down the names of the people they know in these three circles.

This simple activity helps to make children and teens understand the concept of boundaries and how much information can be shared with different groups of people. Since bullies, particularly cyberbullies, exploit personal information, establishing personal boundaries and limiting information such as passwords, photographs and personal details is a useful way to keep them at bay.

3. **Encourage assertiveness**

The first solution that we offer children is to ignore the bully. Ignoring may be useful if one perceives a physical threat from the bully or if the bully is in cyberspace and can be blocked. Assertiveness, on the other hand, is a useful skill to stand up to bullies across situations.

Tell your child that there are usually three ways of responding to situations – submissive, aggressive and assertive. The submissive way of responding includes being passive and tolerating the bully's insults, which may make him/her repeat the behaviour. The aggressive way of responding includes retaliating with physical or verbal aggression to counter the bully, which escalates the bully's hostility. These two ways represent the extremes of responding to situations and are often not effective in countering bullying.

Assertive communication on the other hand offers a means of expressing one's thoughts and feelings in a respectful manner and not in a way that blames the other. It allows the child or teen to tell the bully that what s/he is doing is not acceptable in a calm and confident manner. While asserting yourself, it is important to maintain a calm, even tone, make eye contact and keep an arm's distance from the bully. Parents can teach assertiveness through stories and by enacting scenarios at home with kids. Certain media like short educational films can also depict assertive behaviour to older children and teens.

4. **Build self-esteem and support networks**

Bullies usually target children who lack self-esteem, are easily disturbed or isolated/lonely. Instead of constantly reprimanding children, inculcate self-worth by identifying and building upon their strengths. Entrust them with one responsibility at every age so that they learn to be self-reliant. When children draw their self-esteem from within and not hinge it on what others may think, it can serve as an effective buffer against acts of bullying. Helping children and teens build a support network of trusted friends, classmates and family members to reach out to in difficult situations can help in timely reporting and resolution of any bullying incidents. Instead of venturing alone in situations where s/he may be bullied, the child or teen can be encouraged to move around in a group or have a friend close by to counter the bully. Children who have a strong trusted group of friends are less likely to befriend strangers online or get affected by what random bullies say about them. Good social support systems also foster a sense of self-esteem as children and teens feel accepted and liked. In addition to ensuring a support system, parents need to constantly reinforce that they accept their children unconditionally and are accessible at all times. Since bullying is associated with a sense of shame and weakness, unconditional acceptance by a parent can encourage the child or teen to be honest and proactive in talking about any such instances and seeking timely help.

5. **Report and be proactive**

Encourage children to report any act of bullying from an early age to the appropriate authority. Even if the child or teen is a bystander, s/he should report the incident to the concerned authority. If you feel that your child's reports of being bullied are going unheeded by the authorities and the bullying act is not being adequately addressed, follow it up with the concerned authorities on a personal level. As parents, it is important that we are vigilant about our child's whereabouts and also about the sites and social media s/he is accessing. In cases of cyberbullying, the child or teen should be encouraged to report abuse on the social media platforms and block the bully. Law enforcement authorities can be involved if the child or teen is threatened with physical harm or sensitive information like photographs or videos being leaked publicly.

Timely mental health referral and consultation should be sought in cases where a child or teen is a victim of continuous bullying and suffering from emotional distress or could have engaged in self-harm.

You can also be proactive at a community level by encouraging your child's school, residential locality and workplace to adopt an anti-bullying policy.

To adopt a holistic approach to stop bullying, in addition to standing up to bullies it is important to be aware if your child is engaging in any form of bullying. If your child is behaving aggressively with others or there are any complaints from the school or other parents, pause and think why s/he is doing the same and take active steps to discourage her/him. Bullies are usually children who seek or crave attention. Hence, it is important that parents evaluate whether they are spending adequate time with their child, discouraging any negative attention-seeking behaviour like temper tantrums and encouraging prosocial behaviour. If despite your best efforts, the bullying behaviour and aggression doesn't get resolved, consult a mental health professional.

12

10 Tips to Get Kids to Eat Healthy

Food is one of the most discussed topics among parents today. The conversations range from what the child eats and how much s/he eats to what s/he eats and, most importantly, how much access s/he has to junk foods and sugary beverages. When children are toddlers, parents can control what goes in their tummies but as they grow up, it becomes all about what they like and dislike. These likes and dislikes are influenced by a lot of factors such as parental food habits, friends, media and unique experiences with different foods. If parents keep pandering to these likes and dislikes, they unconsciously reinforce an unhealthy pattern of eating that can lead to a host of health concerns.

Eating healthy is not just about the choice of foods but includes a variety of aspects. These are:

1. The ability to eat independently – More than getting children to eat healthy, it is important to encourage them to eat on their own and not worry whether they will spill or waste.
2. Consuming a balanced diet – This includes a balance of all food groups (carbohydrates, proteins, fats, vitamins and minerals) and eating in moderation.
3. Limiting junk food and sugary beverages – This can be done by designating one day in the week as 'junk food day'.
4. Food portions – This depends on the appetite and levels of satiety, as some children may prefer small meals while others may prefer regular meals.
5. Meal intervals – Small eaters require frequent meals while others may prefer the usual four square meals.

While eating healthy is important, it is also vital that children enjoy the process of eating healthy. Here are ten tips to instil healthy eating habits:

1. Review and modify family eating patterns
Children observe and imbibe numerous habits from their family members. If the family meal menu is centred around the likes and dislikes of family members, then the child will also expect the same. Before getting the child to eat healthy,

make sure that your family meal menu is balanced and healthy. The concept of eating together is a great way to encourage everyone to try whatever is served on the dining table. Eating on time is a vital aspect that is often ignored and erratic mealtimes reinforce unhealthy patterns. Meal timings should be consistent to assist in healthy digestion and assimilation of the food.

2. **Explain the concept of healthy and unhealthy eating habits**
    Educating children about what constitutes healthy/ unhealthy food and how it affects our bodies is vital in encouraging children to make healthier choices and follow through with the new eating habits. For young children, parents can read educational storybooks or get them to engage in art and craft activities by distinguishing foods as healthy and unhealthy. Parents can also animatedly express how healthy food makes our bodies strong and junk food gives us a tummy or tooth ache.

3. **Start small**
    It is wishful thinking to expect a child to suddenly start eating healthy. When you plan the menu, start by incorporating one additional food item.

Encourage your child to eat only one spoon or bite and gradually increase the quantity over a period of time. If your child resists a food item vehemently, don't force or intimidate him/her. Instead, have another healthy alternative ready. Keep your expectations in line with the law of averages and if your child tries the new healthy alternative four out of seven days in the week, perceive it as a big step in the positive direction. Take it slow but keep up the consistent effort.

4. **Incentivize**

Encouragement is a big motivator and helps in propelling one to make greater strides. Each time your child tries a new food item, praise his/her efforts. With young children, you can keep a star chart and give them a star each time they make a healthy choice. At the end of the week, keep a small tangible reward for a certain number of stars earned. You can also organize kids' schedules in such a way that mealtimes are followed by screen or play times. In this way, the screen or play time is seen as a reward for finishing the meal and eating healthy.

5. **Negotiate meal plans**

If children feel invested in an activity, they are more likely to go through with it. Make a list of healthy options for the food menus pertaining to breakfast, lunch and dinner. For each meal per day, have the child select one option that s/he would like the family to have and add another that you would like the family to try. In this way, the child is mentally prepared for what to expect at mealtimes. Being an active part of the decision-making process makes the child more likely to try out the new healthy options.

6. **Be creative**

Nobody likes monotony and meals are no different. The concept of eating out and takeouts has also grown out of boredom associated with home food or the need for variety. Try to add a creative streak while preparing food and planning menus. With a plethora of recipe blogs and videos online, you can prepare and present meals which can be healthy and attractive for kids. If your child is interested in cooking, you can involve him/her in the process. Fireless cooking is also encouraged in summer camps and can be done on the weekends with the child. When children prepare their own meals, they are more likely to eat them too.

7. **Keep mealtimes free of distraction**

In the zeal to get children to eat substantial and healthy meals, parents often fall into the trap of 'screen-feeding' or feeding kids in front of the screen. The child passively keeps putting food in his/her mouth, not recognizing what s/he is eating and how much s/he is eating. The hypothalamus is the part of the brain responsible for regulating hunger and satiety. If children are passively fed for a long period of time, their hypothalamus starts malfunctioning, which leads to overeating and health problems like obesity.

8. **Cheat day or junk day**

Expecting children never to touch junk or sugary beverages is like reaching for the stars at a time when the media makes packaged juices look like healthy energy boosters and shops give free toys with junk food. If that is not enough to entice the child, then peer pressure and serving cakes and cola at birthday parties does the trick. Instead of forcing children to only eat healthy or letting them eat junk whenever they want, follow the middle path of moderation. Most diets have the concept of a cheat day or a day off during the week to eat whatever the person desires. The concept of a cheat day enforces the concept of moderation in the weekly routine. Allow the child to have a junk day which can be preferably a day in the weekend to keep a balance between health and junk. This can also be like an incentive for abiding by the healthy eating routine throughout the week.

9. **Encourage self-help during mealtimes**

Most parents these days get house helpers to become the 'meal assistants' for kids, whether it is putting the meal on the plate, making the child eat or picking up after the child. With this routine children never learn how much to put on the plate, how to eat on their own and, most importantly, how to be self-sufficient. Get your children to take turns to lay the table, learn how to serve and eat independently and clean up after. Don't worry if they spill or serve too much; just treat it like learning another vital life skill.

10. **Finish what's on the plate**

This needs special mention at a time when we are wasting precious resources like water and food. Talk to your children about how much effort it takes in getting the food on the plate – for instance, you can talk about the process of cultivating, harvesting, packaging, cooking and serving the food. Make them aware of the countless people and kids who go hungry every day. Developing respect for people who are involved in providing the food and gratitude towards having access to healthy food is an extremely vital life lesson for children. Make it a rule that everyone will say a prayer or take a minute to be grateful for the food on the table, and that no family member will be allowed to waste or throw food.

While getting your children to eat healthy meals is important, it is also equally important to get them to exercise and digest the food. If your child takes a very long time to finish the meal, do not get impatient. Instead, observe the time s/he takes to complete the meal, and then introduce the concept of finishing the meal five minutes earlier than usual and add it as an additional component on the star chart. For kids who keep food in a corner or are lazy biters, do not mash or puree the food. Instead, get them to do some jaw exercises daily, start with small portions/bites and keep encouraging them to chew their food.

If you notice that your child or adolescent is constantly trying to lose weight despite being healthy, vomiting after every meal or going without food for long intervals, reach out to a mental health professional.

13

Do You Believe in Gender-Sensitive Parenting?

One of the most loved guessing games that expectant parents play is to predict the gender of their unborn baby. Once the child is born, there is a rush to paint the town blue or pink depending on the gender of the child. Then come the dolls or kitchen sets for girls and guns or cars for boys.

'Gender' or the societal expectations of how men and women should look and behave becomes one of the guiding factors in parenting the child. While the notion of factoring gender in the parenting dynamic may help in defining one's identity, it also has a downside. Gender stereotyping or oversimplifying the expectations from males and females often leads to gender discrimination.

For instance, boys are encouraged to be ambitious while girls are encouraged to adjust at every stage of their lives. Gender discrimination fosters a sense of inequality and limitation, which may have a long-lasting impact on self-esteem.

It is vital for parents to create an environment that promotes gender equality and sensitivity to aid the holistic development of the child. Some of the strategies that can help parents achieve this goal are:

1. **Talk about it**

    Young children can be introduced to the concept of gender through the medium of storytelling. Instead of referring to fairy tales where the girl or princess is supposed to be a damsel in distress waiting to be rescued by a boy or Prince Charming, read or tell stories which suggest that qualities are not limited to a particular gender. For instance, a princess can fight off villains on her own and can rescue a prince too.

    For older children, an activity can be done to list out qualities that they consider to be masculine or feminine. You can then talk to them about any gender stereotypes or negative biases that they might have associated with a particular gender. Teenagers can also be encouraged to watch videos that challenge gender biases and promote gender equality.

Holding discussions about gender issues with teenagers and encouraging them to come up with ways in which they can work towards addressing them is a great way to promote gender equality and diversity.

2. **Set an example**
   Children learn by observing their parents. If the father is excused from household chores and encouraged to take it easy after returning from work, they will internalize that it is the woman's role to take on household tasks even if she is tired after her day at work. Be aware of unconsciously promoting gender stereotypes or biases, and actively rectify them. There may be some households in which the father abuses or hits the mother, and it may be normalized by the mother or grandmother. Such perceptions of a certain gender being seen as an aggressor and the other as a victim may promote patterns and cycles of abuse. Make sure that there is mutual respect for everyone and there is no discrimination based on gender roles in the household.

3. **Encourage division of labour**
   This applies to both parents and children. Divide household chores and family responsibilities equally and not based on usual gender roles.

Men and boys can be encouraged to cook and clean for a week, while women and girls can attend to repair work or paying bills for a week and vice versa. Rotate the chores and responsibilities in the house. Working together on household chores also promotes a sense of equality, for instance, the father and mother can both help each other clean up after a meal. Sharing chores and responsibilities also applies to parenting tasks involving feeding, dressing or getting children to do their homework. For example, getting fathers to change diapers and bathing the child and having mothers engage in outdoor sports with the children is a great example of addressing the gender bias in parenting.

4. **Provide equal access and opportunity**
   Raising children in a gender-neutral environment by not segregating colours, toys and activities or providing an atmosphere which allows the child to wear any colour, play with different types of toys and engage in activities that are not defined by gender can help children develop an integrated gender identity and positive gender expression. Instead of shaming a boy for playing with dolls or a tea set, let him learn to be more nurturing and caring. As children grow up, they are expected to choose subjects and

professions based on gender as well. For instance, girls are discouraged from taking up careers that are demanding and involve the family taking a back seat. Encourage children to pursue subjects and later occupations based on abilities and interests. For younger children, this can be done through stories where an animal chooses to be different from others like him/her or by engaging them in artistic activities where they can be given different paper cut-outs of clothes signifying occupations and asked to place the ones they like on a cut-out of a boy or girl. For teenagers, it is vital to make them aware that their professional choices do not need to be based on gender. Biographical accounts and documentaries can help inspire children to take up challenging or unusual professions that defy stereotypes. Discussing issues like glass ceilings in professions and pay disparity with older teenagers can help raise awareness about gender issues in professions and help them look at ways in which these can be addressed.

5. **Use gender-inclusive language**
   While raising children, parents and others often use gender-laden words and phrases such as 'don't cry like a girl' or 'be a man'. These words and phrases have a profound effect on the way children think

about certain genders. Using gender-inclusive or gender-neutral language that removes gender references to describe people helps to counter gender stereotypes and biases.

Examples of gender-inclusive language are:

(a) Using pronouns instead of the gender identity or using 'they/them' as a singular pronoun.
(b) Using gender-neutral terms to describe professions, such as police officer instead of policeman or housekeeper instead of maid/cleaning lady.
(c) Using gender-neutral terms in relationships, like partner, spouse, sibling, child, etc.
(d) Avoiding praising children with phrases like 'good boys' or 'good girls' and instead using phrases such as 'you did a great job'.

Using gender-inclusive language does not mean that gender labels are to be done away with totally. Gender labels can be used when appropriate as long as they do not promote rigid stereotypes.

In addition to the above strategies, it is important to educate and sensitize children that gender is not a binary concept and includes the third gender as well. While talking about the third gender, make sure that you do not attach any stigma or prejudices. For teenagers, it is also important to make them aware of different sexual orientations as an extension of gender expression. Discuss their perceptions about same-sex, opposite-sex and pansexual relationships, and supplement this with information that helps them to develop an open attitude and respect people for the choices that they make.

If your child shows signs of identifying with a particular gender, do not dissuade her/him. Instead, adopt an empathetic stance and make an effort to understand the child's needs and interests and respect the choices that s/he makes. Encourage the child to be who s/he wants to be and not what you or society expects. Unconditional acceptance of a child's choices, gender identity and expression are vital for her/his healthy self-image and self-esteem. At times children may be shamed, trolled or bullied for acting in a way that may not conform to gender-specific behaviour. The child can be taught coping strategies to address such situations by being assertive. Parents can discuss situations with the child and segregate them in terms of those that need to be ignored or blocked and those that need to be responded to. The responses can be in terms of verbal or written counter statements and also about whether a person with authority needs to intervene.

Remember that maintaining open communication and articulating unconditional acceptance are key at every stage of gender-sensitive parenting.

14

Confident Kids

The moments when your child first talks, walks, eats, reads or scribbles on his/her own are celebrated by capturing them through the lens and by writing them down in the baby book. Independence and a sense of mastery is something we all seek as individuals and as parents for our children. Confidence in one's abilities is a reflection of this independence and sense of mastery. The typical approach to parenting is flaw centred, that is, from an early age, we tend to focus more on the things that the child is doing wrong rather than what s/he is doing well. This, along with the constant comparison of the child with others as well as the rush to catch the train of social expectations, leads to him/her imbibing feelings of insecurity and anxiety instead of the sense of confidence that is desired. Recalibrating the parenting approach from flaw focused to ability focused can help parents to achieve the desired goal of raising confident children. This can be done in the following ways:

1. **Encourage positive behaviour**

   Instead of constantly pointing out negative behaviour and saying 'don't do this' and 'don't do that', focus on the tasks that the child is performing well. Praising and encouraging the child for positive and prosocial behaviour communicates a sense of responsibility and mastery. It also helps the child to be open to suggestions for improvement. To help young children gain a sense of mastery, you can create an activity or star chart and ask them to stick or draw pictures of the activities that they need to do in a day. For each day of the week, you can give a star or smiley when a task is completed, and the child can exchange the stars earned for a small tangible reward at the end of the week. Adolescents and young adults can be encouraged to make to-do lists or activity charts by writing down the tasks to be accomplished daily. These tasks can be checked off upon completion to provide an objective analysis of how much work s/he can complete each day and how many tasks s/he can take on in a day without feeling overwhelmed.

2. **Assign responsibilities**

   Today children usually grow up with helpers who are at their beck and call to hand them a glass of water and clean up after them. This along with parents encouraging children only to focus on academics or co-curricular activities leads to children taking on selective responsibilities and being constantly dependent on others. This method of 'delegating one's responsibilities to others' does not work when children leave their homes to join a boarding school or a university hostel or later a job, where they are required to multitask and take on multiple responsibilities. If children are assigned responsibilities from an early age, they learn to manage multiple fronts at a time, which helps them to be confident, responsible and adaptable in the face of any challenge or situation. This can be done by involving children in household chores from an early age and letting them handle the responsibility on their own. The chores can be added as an activity/ task in their daily schedule so that it becomes a habit. Make sure that responsibilities are distributed among family members so that the child does not feel that s/he is being singled out.

3. Encourage decision-making and inculcate problem-solving skills

Adapting to any situation is key to feeling confident. The best way to make children adaptable and flexible is by encouraging them to learn the art of decision-making from an early age and teaching them problem-solving skills. Puzzles, mazes and blocks can be a starting point to introduce decision-making and problem-solving to toddlers. Later, children can be encouraged to pick out clothes, books and toys that they would like to wear. Older children can be encouraged to plan their daily schedules or choose subjects that will determine the courses that they would like to pursue. For situations that may cause stress or anxiety, children and adolescents can be taught specific decision-balancing and problem-solving skills. Decision-balancing refers to weighing pros and cons as well as reflecting upon short-term and long-term consequences of their responses/actions. Problem-solving skills involve clearly defining the problem or concern at hand, brainstorming about the possible solutions, choosing a viable solution through decision-balancing and then reviewing whether the solution helps in resolving the problem. If the solution is effective, then it can be used in similar situations but if it is not, then one can go back to the possible solutions and come up with an alternative method.

4. **Identify and build strengths**

Each child has unique attributes, talents and strengths, which can be observed by spending time or listening to him/her. Some children may be academically oriented, while others may excel in a sport or have an artistic ability. Instead of constantly comparing children with other children and pushing them to live up to societal standards, focus on nurturing their unique talents and strengths. Focusing on abilities fosters self-esteem, and also helps to counter self-doubt, sadness and anxiety. From a young age, parents can help children identify their strengths through activities like making a collage about the things that the child is interested in and is good at. These can be depicted in the form of picture cut-outs, drawings or text. Adolescents can be encouraged to make a list of their abilities/ strengths and of the aspects they would like to strengthen. Enrolling children in special classes after school can also be a way of identifying abilities/ talents, but it is important to stick to one to two special classes at a time to maintain focus. A sound knowledge about one's skills and abilities can also help determine future career choices.

5. **Adopt a holistic approach to boost self-esteem**

While identifying and building strengths is important, it is also vital that children are able to develop strengths across various aspects that are linked to their self and sense of happiness. This can be done by getting them to make a self-chart. You can use the pizza or pie analogy – just like a pizza or pie is divided into many slices to help us eat it easily and relish it, we can derive happiness and confidence from many aspects. Ask the child to make a circle or a confidence/happiness pizza and divide it into segments/slices pertaining to friends, family, studies, interests, exercise, etc. Now ask him/her what are the things that are working well in each of these domains – for instance, s/he may be able to spend time with parents and have friends, or be able to finish school assignments on time. Then ask about what can be improved in each of these domains – for instance, s/he could enrol in a class to develop an interest/hobby or meet friends more often. Through this activity, the child becomes aware that s/he is managing several aspects well and concerns with one aspect doesn't translate into a sense of failure or lack of confidence. This chart can also be used to identify the areas where the child's confidence is lacking and can be built up using problem-solving skills.

6. **Instil communication and public-speaking skills**
The ability to express oneself and communicate effectively boosts confidence. Young children can be taught communication skills through the art of storytelling. Inflections in parental speech help children understand how different emotions are communicated. Parents can encourage children from an early age to look at different pictures and talk about what they think is happening in the picture or make a story around it. Older children can be presented with situations in the form of role plays and asked to improvise what the characters would say or how they would respond to those situations. Assertive communication can be taught through such role plays, where the child can be encouraged to say no or express views in a respectful manner. This can be done by teaching the 'communication sandwich approach' and the 'broken record technique'. The communication sandwich approach involves starting a conversation with a positive

statement about the other person to engage them, then communicating the message one wants to convey, and closing on a positive note. The broken record technique refers to communicating the same message over and over again without raising one's voice. Public-speaking skills can be taught by encouraging the child to read out lines in front of a mirror and participate in drama classes or by using the 'reader's theatre approach' in which the child along with family members can enact a story and read out dialogues from a storybook.

7. **Foster optimism and positive thinking**

Confidence in one's demeanour springs from a positive or optimistic mindset. This includes the ability to counter negative thoughts, specifically pertaining to self-doubt. Positive thinking and an optimistic mindset can be fostered in a number of ways. The first involves parents modelling positivity. If as a parent we always focus on negative aspects about situations and people, then children imbibe the same mindset. However, if a parent focuses on appreciating the positives in situations and people, then children do the same. The second way to foster positivity involves teaching the child problem-solving or adopting a solution-based approach.

Whenever the child has a negative thought or gets frustrated with a situation, encourage him/her to come up with possible solutions to address the concern. The third way to foster positivity is to teach the child 'disputation skills' or countering the negative thought by listing the points against it. For instance, if a child keeps saying that 'nobody wants to be his/her friend', you can encourage him/her to think of peers/cousins who have been friendly, and then point out that at times children may not play exclusively with him/her but that does not mean that s/he does not have any friends. A fourth way to counter negative thoughts is to think of what can be the best, worst and likely outcomes. This approach can be taught to children who are eight years old and above. Looking at the best, worst and likely scenarios helps children to avoid jumping to worst-case scenarios and catastrophizing about situations.

When raising confident children it is vital to understand that 'confidence' is a dynamic construct and there may be times when the child feels overwhelmed. In those circumstances, it is important to encourage the child to seek help and remind the child of the instances when s/he was able to turn a difficult situation around. There also may be instances when children confuse confidence with a 'sense of superiority'. Hence, it is critical that parents make children understand that confidence is an ability to manage our thoughts, feelings and actions effectively while being grounded.

15

10 Ways to Manage Emotions

Most conversations start with the conventional 'how are you?' and what follows is a myriad of responses based on the emotion that one is experiencing. Emotions are an integral part of our lives and affect the way we think and behave in various situations. The palette of our lives is coloured with a variety of emotions including happiness, sadness, anger, anxiety and disgust to name a few. Each of these emotions has a survival value to help us cope with different situations. Just like a balanced diet is essential for a healthy body, balanced emotional regulation is the secret to a healthy mind. The ability to achieve this balance by managing one's emotions and those of others is known as 'emotional intelligence'. The essentials skills that underscore emotional intelligence constitute self-awareness or being aware of one's emotions, self-regulation or the ability to manage emotions appropriately, motivation or a commitment to improve oneself and social/interpersonal skills to manage others' emotions effectively. As parents, it is vital that we strive to raise emotionally intelligent children by nurturing these skills.

Here are ten ways in which you can teach and help your children to effectively manage emotions and grow into emotionally intelligent adults:

1. Relaxation routine

Teaching children to set aside some time for relaxing or winding down during the day is a vital life skill. Relaxation helps to alleviate anxiety and keep anger at bay. It also helps to focus the mind, which is essential to excel in any aspect of life, be it academics, sports or one's profession at a later stage. Simple breathing exercises can be taught from an early age and parents can do them along with the child as a part of family relaxation time. For young children, you can make the breathing exercises fun by introducing the concept of a 'belly buddy' – a small soft toy which they keep in their lap or on their bellies when they lie down, who jumps up when the child breathes in. For older children, you can combine a simple imagery exercise with deep breathing. You can use specific imagery to deal with situations that evoke fear/anxiety or anger. For instance, if a child has a fear of giving exams or tests, ask him/her to imagine walking towards the examination room calmly. Then focus on the paper being handed over by the teacher which has all the questions that s/he has prepared. Ask the child to imagine him/herself solving all the questions confidently and handing over the paper.

2. Mindfulness

This is the ability to be aware of our thoughts, feelings and actions in the present moment without being overwhelmed by them. Being mindful enhances self-awareness, which is an important component of emotional intelligence. Inculcating mindfulness from an early age helps children become more aware of their feelings and helps them to manage these feelings effectively. A simple mindfulness exercise, which can be taught and used across age groups, is the STOP exercise. The child is taught to momentarily pause whatever s/he is engaged in (stop), take a breath to focus on the breathing sensation (take a breath), acknowledge and note the thoughts and feelings within (observe) and then proceed with whatever s/he was doing (proceed).

This simple exercise helps us acknowledge our thoughts and feelings without repressing or getting overwhelmed by them.

3. **Physical exercise**
There is an innate connection between the mind and body. We express the emotions we feel through the body via facial expressions and gestures. Engaging in routine physical activity and exercise releases endorphins and gives rise to feelings of happiness and positivity. It also provides an outlet for negative emotions like anxiety and anger. For instance, physical activity helps to calm children who are prone to anxiety and allows children who are prone to aggression to channelize their pent-up anger and energy in a positive way.

4. **Diaries and artwork**
Maintaining personal diaries is an age-old tool to give expression to one's thoughts and feelings. Young children can be initiated into the concept of expressing their thoughts and feelings through artistically depicting them and using various colours for different emotions such as black for sadness, red for anger, yellow for happiness, etc. Older children can be encouraged to write about their

day by focusing on their thoughts and feelings. Maintaining daily diary records facilitates emotional catharsis and provides an outlet to emotions and feelings one may hesitate to share with another but feels the need to vent. Technological options for the traditional diary such as online diaries, writing software, social media and blogs provide a more public platform to express feelings and should be used with discretion.

5. **Activity charts and mastery charts**
Negative emotions are underscored by feelings of loss of control and uncertainty. Having children and adolescents follow a daily routine with a set of activities helps to add a degree of order. Getting the child to check off each activity once it is done provides positive feedback and a sense of mastery, which makes the child feel better about him/herself. For younger children, you can ask them to indicate how they felt about doing the different activities by making a smiley or emoticon displaying happiness, sadness, anger or fear. This can help identify the areas that may need to be addressed by the parents to help the child feel better. For older children, adolescents and adults, activity and mastery charts evolve into

tools of time management and self-improvement, which underscore the motivational component of emotional intelligence.

6. **Stories, props and role play**

Expressing feelings is an important element of managing emotions. Reading stories which talk about different emotions and asking children how different characters may be feeling at different points of a story is a creative way to get them to identify their own feelings and those of others. Creative storytelling is another means by which children can be encouraged to understand the link between thoughts, feelings and actions and taught about different ways to manage emotions better. Finger and hand puppets make great props for encouraging children to become aware of different feelings and learn ways of expressing them better. For adolescents, drama and role play serve as tools to teach coping methods like assertiveness, communication and social skills.

7. **Coping skills**

Teaching vital coping skills to children and adolescents can help them manage their own emotions and those of others effectively. These include:

(a) **Distraction** or shifting the focus away from the negative emotion to neutral activities. This is particularly useful in reducing emotional intensity at times when one may feel overwhelmed with anxiety, anger or sadness.

(b) **Problem-solving** or thinking divergently about an issue. This can help resolve it effectively, and thus address the negative emotions associated with it. Clearly defining a problem, brainstorming about the possible alternatives, choosing the most viable alternative and testing it can help manage anxiety and anger-provoking situations efficiently. Problem-solving can also evolve into goal-setting exercises later in life.

(c) **Assertiveness** or the ability to express your beliefs and emotions without being disrespectful to others. Children can be taught to be assertive by first distinguishing between aggressive, submissive and assertive behaviour, and then encouraging them to maintain eye contact and an even tone while putting their point across.

8. Countering negative thoughts

Every feeling feeds into a thought and vice versa. Becoming aware of negative thinking patterns by recording them helps one identify situations which trigger and evoke negative emotions. Challenging negative thoughts is a skill which can be taught to older children and adolescents. The first step to counter a negative thought is to evaluate whether something can be done about it or not. If one cannot do anything about it, it is better to disengage and distract oneself. On the other hand, if you feel something can be done about it, you can use problem-solving skills. Another approach to countering negative thoughts is evaluating whether they are valid or not by putting down points in favour and against them. If one is able to challenge negative thoughts effectively, they lose the power to make one feel negative.

9. **Social skills**

These comprise teaching communication, negotiation, cooperation and collaboration. Teaching children to develop listening skills is the first step. Narrating stories and asking the child questions about the same sets the foundation for listening skills and paraphrasing. While communicating with others, encourage children to start with a note of appreciation, followed by raising the point of concern. Older children can be taught skills of 'reflection' or mirroring the content and emotion communicated by another, and 'summarizing' the content of conversations at the end. Non-verbal communication should also be emphasized from an early age by encouraging children to maintain eye contact, an open posture and an even tone while talking to another person. Skills pertaining to collaboration and cooperation can be taught through team-building games and activities.

10. **Embracing chores and social cause**
Developing and communicating 'empathy' or the ability to feel with another is critical to managing emotions. If one is able to extend oneself beyond the realm of the self and appreciate others' emotions and struggles, one matures and grows emotionally by leaps and bounds. Getting children to do home chores from an early age is a great way to develop empathy for their parents and helpers. It also helps them grow above likes and dislikes, and not get disturbed emotionally if they are assigned tasks that they do not wish to do or struggle with. Getting children to extend themselves and become socially responsible is a great way to develop empathy. Committing to any small cause helps the child feel motivated to move beyond the self, cooperate with

others and feel positive – all of which make him/her socially and emotionally intelligent. If at any point the child feels low, s/he can use the experience of working towards a cause as a reality check that there are others who may be struggling too but are taking steps to overcome their circumstances.

Despite your best efforts if your child is feeling anxious or sad, having thoughts of helplessness, hopelessness and worthlessness and is experiencing symptoms (palpitations, sweating, shortness of breath, irritability, headaches, nausea, sleep disturbances, increased/reduced appetite, etc.) which do not have any medical basis, then it is vital to consult a mental health professional.

As you strive to raise an emotionally intelligent child, remember that emotions are dynamic by nature and can overwhelm anyone at some point in life. Instead of resisting negative emotions, embrace them as springboards for growth and keep teaching your child ways to manage them effectively.

16

Raising Resilient Kids

Aren't we all guilty of chasing achievement and avoiding discomfort? This has also percolated into the way we parent our children. We seek to provide them with things even before they express a desire for them. From the day the child enters playschool, there is a push to 'perform par excellence' in academic and co-curricular activities. The child grows up to believe that success is to be celebrated and failure to be avoided. It further strengthens the belief that success is the key to social acceptance and people do not want to associate with failure. This approach of chasing success may serve well to pursue and achieve goals but it does not prepare the child to cope with adversity. Instead of providing children with algorithms to achieve success, we need to encourage our children to adopt a heuristic approach to navigate through life and equip them with resilience.

Resilience simply defined is the ability to cope with any adversity. It is like an inner reservoir of strength, which the person can draw from when s/he faces any challenge that threatens his/her well-being. It is vital to inculcate resilience in our kids from an early age. Here are some ways in which you can make your children resilient:

Normalize failure

Talk to your children about the importance of both success and failure. Failure is not something to be avoided or feared but is an opportunity to reflect on how one could have done things differently. It is vital to educate children that one may not feel good about oneself on failing but it is not a reflection of one's ability. Stories are a great way to make children understand the concepts of success and failure. Make sure that you read books in which the central character meets with challenges and failures from time to time but is able to come up with ways of resolving and overcoming them.

For older children, biographies and human narratives of handling failures can be a great way to destigmatize failure. They can be encouraged to read or watch documentaries of inspirational people and discuss what they liked or lessons they could imbibe in their life.

Focus on abilities

We all have a tendency to focus on weaknesses or reprimand children when they don't behave in a certain way or live up to our and societal expectations. This sets the stage for poor self-esteem and may lead to the child crumbling under pressure or adversity. Instead, if the child is made aware of his/her abilities and encouraged to draw from his/her strengths, s/he will feel more confident in handling any crisis. This can be done with a simple daily exercise. Younger children can be encouraged to think of one thing that they like about themselves in the morning and evening. Older children can be encouraged to list their abilities and go over that list in the morning and evening or write down one ability or competency daily in the morning and evening. This simple exercise helps one to become more aware of one's strengths and develop a positive attitude, which can be utilized in adversity.

The balancing act

There are different aspects to the self. For instance, relationships with family, friends and romantic partner, work, personal interests, etc. We all assign a degree of importance to each of them, which may change from time to time. If we attach too much importance to one aspect of the self, we risk feeling dejected and breaking down when things do not go as planned or expected in that domain. For instance, we may push our child to get a certain percentage in his/her examinations, resulting in him/her placing too much emphasis on marks and basing his/her self-esteem on it. If s/he performs poorly in an exam or fails, it may shatter him/her mentally. Balancing the different aspects of our self in terms of the importance that we assign to them can help a person stay equipoised in times of adversity. If the child who performs poorly in exams bases equal importance on sports, co-curricular activities, friends and academics, s/he may feel bad about performing poorly but may not be shattered as s/he has good friends to support him/her or is able to play a sport well.

As mentioned before, you can help children learn to balance different aspects of their self and lives by asking them to draw a circle on a paper and imagine it to be a pie, then draw segments of the slices of the pie representing different aspects that matter to him/her and assign a percentage of importance to each of these in a balanced way. For instance, friends – 20 per cent, academics – 30 per cent, sports – 20 per cent, hobbies – 20 per cent, family – 20 per cent, etc.

Developing a sense of mastery

There is a parental tendency of doing things for the child from an early age, which makes him/her dependent. Instead of doing things for the child or making decisions for him/her, let him/her take initiative and make mistakes. It is important for the child to learn from mistakes and ride out the frustration. This can be done from an early age by telling children to be responsible for household chores such as picking up the toys after they finish playing, etc. Household chores are a great way to teach the child to rise above likes and dislikes, which is an essential feature of being resilient. For small children, you can give them a star and verbal appreciation every time they are able to follow through with a task. For older children, you can use household chores and summer jobs as means of earning a stipend and teaching dignity of labour. Each time the child does something well or makes decisions, it gives him/her a sense of competence and mastery, which feeds into the belief that one can rely on oneself to overcome challenging tasks.

Problem-solving skills

Teaching children how to solve problems or deal with challenging situations is key to developing resilience. Small children can be taught by presenting problem scenarios from a story and then asking them to come up with different solutions to resolve it. For older children, you can teach them to write any problem that they may have encountered and then brainstorm the various solutions that can be used to resolve it. They should choose the most viable solution on the basis of pros and cons and try it out. If it doesn't resolve the problem, then they should go back to the list of solutions and try something else. Thinking divergently about a problem/situation develops mental flexibility, which is an essential component of resilience. Whenever the child is effectively able to overcome a problem or adversity, s/he can note it down in a competence diary, so that it can be used as a reference point in managing similar circumstances.

Countering negative thoughts

Giving in to negative thoughts and beliefs can cripple our ability to bounce back from adversity. Inculcating skills which can help the child counter negative thoughts is essential for mental fortitude. Whenever the child encounters a difficult situation, ask him/her to write down 'what is the best that can happen', 'what is the worst that can happen' and 'what is likely to happen'. This helps him/her to be more realistic about the situation at hand and makes the situation appear less threatening than it is perceived to be. For instance, the child who fails in a board exam and feels like s/he should resort to self-harm can reason that the worst that can happen is 'people will heckle at him/her and s/he may have to repeat a class', the best scenario is 'nobody will say anything and s/he will give the exam again and pass with good marks' and a likely scenario is that 'some people may heckle but s/he can give the paper again and pass the exam'. Another way to counter negative thoughts is to list the evidence for and against the thought. For instance, in the failing scenario the child may think 's/he is a failure'. The evidence for it may be 's/he failed this exam' but the evidence against can be 's/he has succeeded in so many exams before, and is good at sports', and so s/he cannot be labelled as a 'failure'.

Making bucket lists

Making a list of goals or experiences that you would like to have can serve as a motivation to move ahead while facing a difficult situation. We may think that our life has a sole purpose, but the truth is that we need to keep inventing these purposes from time to time. Encourage the child to make a bucket list and keep adding things to it.

Committing to social causes which go beyond self-interest is an important component of making the bucket list as it can help counter feelings of emptiness that may set in once personal goals or material needs are fulfilled.

Finding your zen

An important part of resilience is the ability to de-stress. Help your child identify ways in which s/he can cope with stress. Some of these are distracting oneself when feeling overwhelmed by talking to a friend/family member or indulging in something of interest. The child can be encouraged to make a list of things which help him/her calm down such as drawing, listening to music, dancing, etc. Some parents may use praying or chanting to summon the strength to deal with difficult situations and can teach their children to do the same. Having a daily routine with physical exercise and relaxation exercises/breathing exercises helps to provide a sense of stability and fortitude to combat daily stressors.

Support system

Although self-reliance is an important element of resilience, there are times when we may not be able to help ourselves and require support to tide over adversity. Help the child identify family and friends who s/he can reach out to in times of need. Make sure that these people exude warmth, are trustworthy and have a positive outlook. In addition to helping the child identify persons who constitute his/her support network, make sure you communicate that reaching out to people in times of adversity is not a sign of weakness.

A list of different helplines such as those that address mental health emergencies and concerns can be put up on a wall or in an accessible location in the house. Having a good support system gives a sense of belonging, which counters feelings of isolation and loneliness.

As you seek to make your child resilient, make sure that you serve as a model and practise what you preach. Keep the channels of communication open and encourage the child to communicate his/her thoughts and feelings. Make sure to remind your children that change is the only constant in life and that one has to keep adapting oneself and adding to one's inner resources. While being resilient may help one to bounce back from adversity, there may be times when despite having all the inner strength and resources, your child may break down emotionally and is unable to handle situations. In those times it is important to reach out to a mental health professional and not to be disheartened.

17

Parenting Lessons from Festivals

India is a land of festivals. Even though coronavirus has played spoilsport this year, dampening our festive spirits, our schools are leaving no stone unturned to instil the spirit of festivity in our children! From Eid to Christmas and from Gurpurab and Baisakhi to Pongal, children can learn invaluable lessons from Indian festivals.

Last year, true to the spirit of Vijayadashmi, our society complex had a Ramlila put up by the children. Since my son was just five years old then, he was offered the role of a rakshasa in Ravana's sena. Apart from delighting in my son's first stage performance, something else struck a chord. The girl who was playing the role of Ravana had lost her father just days before the Ramlila performance. She is all of thirteen but displayed courage and maturity much beyond her age.

Instead of breaking down or backing out, she followed through with her commitment towards participating in the show and making it a grand success. The organizers lauded her embodiment of the spirit of the Ramayana, of putting duty before anything else and overcoming adversity. The curtain had dropped but the vision of the brave thirteen-year-old who overcame her grief to evoke wonder in the hearts of the audience stayed with me. This is what festivals teach us too – duty before self and commitment.

Here are nine lessons that children can learn from Indian festivals:

1. The power of prayer

Numerous mantras are chanted during puja rituals. Having children learn and recite mantras can help sharpen their cognitive abilities. The forehead or prefrontal part of our brain is the seat of attention, concentration, problem-solving and decision-making. There are numerous researches which show that chanting a mantra as simple as Aum helps to stimulate the prefrontal part of the brain and thereby improves attention and concentration and enhances learning ability. Saying grace during Christmas is a beautiful way to thank the Lord and can help children recount their blessings, which they take for granted. Harvest festivals such as Baisakhi, Onam and Pongal are good opportunities to teach kids to be grateful for the food on the table. Encourage children to pray not only for their families and friends before meals but also for the farmers who till the land. In their morning and night prayers they can include the health workers working at the front lines during the pandemic and the soldiers keeping our country safe.

2. **Unity and harmony**

Whether it is the story of how the gods combined their powers to give birth to Goddess Durga to kill Mahishasura or how the army of vanaras worked in unison to construct a bridge and fight the asuras, working together as a team towards common goals is a vital life skill. At every stage of life we have to set aside our ego from time to time and work as a team. Through mythological stories and by delegating tasks pertaining to cleaning the house, wrapping gifts or decorating the house during festivals such as Eid or Christmas, children can be encouraged to pitch in and learn the art of working together.

3. **Optimism and problem-solving**

Mythological stories such as the Ramayana serve as great tools for teaching optimism and problem-solving skills. If you reflect on the story, Rama, Sita and Lakshmana faced many adversities, such as being banished to the forest and the encounter with Ravana. At each step, all the characters exhibited the ability to accept adversity with optimism and solve problems effectively. For instance, Rama forged a relationship with Sugriva, built the bridge across the ocean and tried having a dialogue with Ravana before deciding to go to war and eventually defeating him. Using mythological stories related to festivals acts as an educational experience and helps children imbibe vital skills.

Stories from the Bible and the Guru Granth Sahib teach us about the goodness in each of us and how to be kind to every living being. Festivals are a perfect time to revisit these stories and teach your child about the importance of looking at the brighter side.

4. Respect for elders

Diwali is a time when people of all ages come together to celebrate. It provides the perfect setting to encourage children to learn values of humility, extend a helping hand, speak politely and respect elders. Children can learn a lot from elders, who are storehouses of wisdom and experience. Encouraging children to touch elders' feet is a small but significant step. Bowing down in front of a person is a symbol of surrendering the ego and receiving love, blessings and positive vibrations. Just asking children to respect elders is not enough. You need to serve as a positive role model every step of the way to ensure the message hits home.

5. **Making the right choices**

Many Hindu mythological stories are centred around rakshasas doing penance to appease Lord Shiva for the boon of immortality and then misusing the boon for personal gain. These simple stories exhibit how our choices shape our destinies, and how easily a boon can become a bane. Just the other day my son asked me, 'Why do we need to burn Ravana again and again? Can't he just die for once?' The symbolism of Ravana denotes two aspects of our lives – the negative tendencies or habits we have and the bad choices we make. I told my son that every year we keep feeling negative about something or the other and make bad choices from time to time. Festivals like Dussehra, Gurpurab and Christmas give us the opportunity to become aware of our negativity and re-evaluate our choices. They help us to choose more wisely and better ourselves every year.

6. **Cleanliness**

Diwali is the one time of the year when people clean every neglected nook and cranny to usher in Goddess Lakshmi into their homes. It is also the best time to teach children the importance of cleaning not only your own homes but also working towards a clean tomorrow. By encouraging children to avoid crackers, choose earthen diyas, make lanterns from old newspapers and use fresh flowers and organic colours (for rangoli), you can drive home the message about the use of biodegradable materials, recycling and encouraging small artisans. In addition to cleaning the outside, it is also vital to get children to look within and clean their minds and hearts – a simple way to get them to think about what it is that they would like to change within or ways in which we can learn to think and feel better.

7. **The gift of health**

Gifts are something adults and children look forward to. Instead of gifting sugary treats and plastic items, make it a point to choose healthy alternatives like fruits, plants and steel. Encourage children to think of healthy and environment-friendly gifts so that they continue to make healthier choices later in life as well. Instead of buying a box of candy and adding another plastic toy to your child's collection, encourage him/her to think of a healthy and eco-friendly alternative. Remember, the best way to learn is to be a part of the process.

8. **Charity**

Charity is not just about giving money to the needy but also about spending time with them and giving them respect. Diwali can be one occasion to get your child to spend time with underprivileged children. While celebrating Gurpurab, Sikhs engage in seva or selfless service to feed the poor. Money is given to the needy during Eid celebrations. Christians distribute gifts to the homeless and needy to spread cheer during Christmas. During the festivities, you can read out stories to children about helping people in need and engage them in making cards, distributing food and selecting and wrapping gifts for them. You can encourage them to continue distributing food packets and engaging in activities such as storytelling for underprivileged children throughout the year as an extension of the lessons they learned during the festive period.

9. **Respect for women**

Praying to the goddess and celebrating the feminine energy is a central theme in festivals like Navratri and Diwali. On the one hand, we seek the blessings of the goddess and adorn her in the best jewels and finery in temples, but on the other we disrespect women on a day-to-day basis. Festivals can serve as a platform to teach children to respect and value women. This can be done through small acts like encouraging boys to help in puja rituals, particularly ones like Ashtami and Navami puja. Positive stories from mythology such as the annihilation of Mahishasura at the hands of Goddess Durga or the courage displayed by Sita in raising Luv and Kusha practically as a single parent can help to emphasize the positive role women play in our cultural heritage.

So this time when you celebrate festivals, make sure to gift your children some valuable life lessons by making them a part of the experience and not mere spectators.

18

Traditional Wisdom for Young Parents

Remember your childhood days when you looked forward to getting wet in the rain, playing hopscotch on the street and spending time with grandparents? Cut to the millennial reality where your children are shuffling between after-school classes, television, Xbox and social media. Modern parents struggle to keep a tab on their child from a very young age.

Just the other day a young mother in my apartment complex was asking for recommendations about preschools. While I was enumerating the pros of the preschool my daughter attends, she abruptly stopped me to ask whether the school has a live feed for parents. When I shook my head, she went on to emphasize how important it was to monitor every moment of the child, teachers and help staff. Though I agree with the concept of schools having cameras for 'authorities' to monitor the environment better, I am baffled with the amount of control parents seek to exercise over their children. What they don't realize is that planning every second of their child's life and monitoring their every move is counterproductive to a child's growth and development.

A healthier approach to parenting is to maintain the balance. A mix of traditional and modern parenting practices can help achieve this balance and propel children towards health, resilience and confidence. While the millennial parent is well acquainted with the modern parenting mantras, reflecting on these five traditional ones may help provide new insights to raising happy children:

Home remedies

The first traditional parenting mantra involves use of home remedies. This is in line with the organic revolution that we see unfolding around us. Over the years we have been aping Western practices blindly – breastfeeding is traded for bottles of formula milk and baby food in a box is thought to have more nutrients than freshly prepared meals. While these practices may be more convenient, they are not necessarily beneficial.

Every household in India is blessed with their

own set of natural hacks, passed down through the generations. These home remedies are organic/natural and are much more beneficial for preserving our health and well-being as compared to chemical alternatives. For instance, asafoetida or hing helps to soothe colic in infants and children and herbs like brahmi have been found to facilitate cognitive development. So just as you cherish the recipes that are handed down by your mothers and grandmothers, embrace traditional remedies as well so that you can ensure that your child also receives 'the gift of health' in today's fast-moving day and age.

Outdoor play

The second mantra is earthing or encouraging the child to spend time outdoors, close to nature and the environment. Millennial parents today encourage their children to lead highly sanitized lives, and are often found rubbing sanitizer on the child's hands with a Macbethian fervour and obsessing about keeping their children close to an air purifier. There is an apron for painting, kinetic sand as an alternative to real sand and play dough as an alternative to mud.

What the modern parent fails to recognize is that oversanitization compromises the immunity of a child. A recent research shows that children who suck their thumbs and bite their nails are less likely to suffer from allergies, because they are exposed to microbes and develop immunity against allergens. Nothing thrives in captivity, and the same is true for children.

Parks and outdoor play areas provide a great tactile learning experience replete with varied textures to stimulate young minds. Physical activity aids physical and mental health by releasing endorphins or feel-good hormones. Children who are engaged in outdoor games and sports have more stamina than those sitting in front of an electronic babysitter. Parents can have conversations about different aspects of the environment such as trees or flowers in a park to add to the child's general fund of knowledge and sharpen his/her observation skills. I remember as a child my brother and I would spend time with my maternal grandfather. He would take us to the park and tell us about the different varieties of trees and flowers that we saw there. While I have forgotten many facts that I may have read in textbooks, the knowledge that I garnered during those visits is etched in my memory.

Adapting to change
Adapting to change is a vital life skill which is in short supply in the present day and age. Parents often schedule

'play dates' to help children socialize with other children and learn concepts like 'sharing is caring'. What they don't realize is that most of these play dates are restricted to a certain group of children who have been vetted by the parents as 'positive influences'. While these structured dates may allow children to make friends with certain children, they aren't the best means of inculcating social skills. Traditional parenting practices focused on exposing children to a variety of social situations. For instance, grandparents would take children to the park and encourage them to play with all the kids. There were trips to places like open vegetable markets, the post office, banks, etc. and children were encouraged to greet people and help in selecting vegetables, paste a stamp on the letter and push it into the cylindrical red postbox. Such instances of exposing children to different play and social situations with different groups of people helps them to learn the art of communicating with people of diverse temperaments and interests. The child also learns to stand up for him/herself when confronted with a difficult child/situation. These experiences facilitate creative problem-solving which helps in effective handling of any situation/person. Today intelligence is no longer seen as how well you score on an IQ test but as how well you can adapt to your environment.

Engage kids in chores

While adapting to any situation is vital, it is also important to learn how to be resilient. This brings us to the fourth mantra of engaging children in household chores. With didis and bhaiyas being at parents' beck and call, it is no wonder that children also start depending on the house help for anything and everything. This habit of having another attend to their daily needs and chores feeds into the idea that one should only do the work they like and leave the work that they do not like for someone else.

Traditional parenting methods focused on assigning certain responsibilities to everyone in the family, whether they liked it or not. During my summer holidays, my maternal grandmother would delegate different household chores to each grandchild and pay us some money after we completed the task. We would then buy ourselves a chocolate or a packet of chips, which was something to look forward to. However, at times we were asked to do a task that we didn't like or pulled up for being tardy. It all seemed mundane back then, but in hindsight the whole experience was a valuable life lesson.

Assigning chores translates into helping the child learn to be responsible. Completion of a chore gives him/her a sense of competence and builds self-esteem. When additional chores are added to the routine, the child learns the art of time management. There may be times when the child is not able to carry out tasks or resents some tasks, but if s/he is still able to stick it out, s/he learns the art of resilience. Resilience is key to leading a successful life. Success is not about the times you win but about how often you are able to pick yourself up after a failure and not give up on yourself. A seventy-five-year-old Harvard Grant study also validates that children who engage in household chores are more likely to be successful in life.

Acceptance

The last and most important traditional parenting mantra is acceptance. Life in the present day is full of expectations. Parents have high expectations of their children from day one. Most often these expectations are fuelled by societal expectations. We have a checklist for every age, and in case the child makes mistakes and falls short of what is expected of him/her, we are quick to express our disappointment. Most parents forget that while growing up, the best gift that their grandparents gave them was unconditional love and acceptance.

Just the other day I read an article about a mother who had posted online that even though her son did not get a high score in the board exams, she was still proud that he had coped well with the stress of examination and not given up. It was refreshing to see that she had accepted her son's struggle and celebrated his endurance. It is important to recognize that every child is unique and should be encouraged to be the best version of him/herself. If as parents we accept our child's limitations in the same way we accept his/her abilities, we can help him/her achieve his/her highest potential.

Even though traditions may seem like a thing of the past, the wisdom they hold has the power to transform the future of our children.

19

Kids and Abuse

Secrets have a unique quality about them. They can rouse a myriad of emotions within us – curiosity, excitement, guilt, shame, sadness. While we all keep secrets, some have a high cost, both physically and emotionally. One such secret is 'abuse'. Every day newspapers and WhatsApp videos are buzzing with incidents ranging from a maid physically abusing a child to a teacher molesting a student to, worst of all, a father sexually molesting his own daughter. We respond by having angry exchanges with family, friends and colleagues and blaming everyone from unreliable helpers to the police to the government. As parents we respond by becoming paranoid about the safety of our children and go to all lengths to ensure that our child is protected from any abuse. We install CCTV cameras to monitor the maid, request our net-savvy friends for tips to block objectionable material and install apps which can help track the child's location. These may be great ways to safeguard children, but the most vital element is for parents to talk about abuse with their children.

Awareness is the first step to ensure that a child understands what abuse is and how s/he can prevent or report abuse. Talking about abuse, just like talking about sex, isn't easy. There is no standard template for all ages since the level of maturity is different across age groups and there is a fine line between information and too much information. The way forward is to present the information based on the child's age and maturity level.

Toddlers and children (3 to 8 years)

The concept of 'morality' or the understanding of good and bad is limited to avoiding punishment from authority figures like parents, teachers, etc. and behaving in a manner which is pleasing to the authority figure. For instance, if a helper is abusing a child behind the parents' back and threatening him/her not to tell the parents, the child is less likely to report the incident as s/he wants to avoid punishment from the helper. The topics to be discussed with the child should include the concept of good touch and bad touch, physical boundaries, talking about any unpleasant experiences with parents/trusted adults, not accepting candy/gifts from strangers and not going alone anywhere.

The strategies or ways to talk to children of this age group include:

- **Pictures, drawings and videos** – Children at this age are receptive to everything visual and the best way to talk to them about sensitive information is through pictures, drawings or videos. Board books with parts of the body can be used to have a discussion about different parts of the body which cannot be touched by anyone apart from parents or trusted adults. Children at this age also imbibe a lot of things from the screen, particularly from the videos that they watch, often unsupervised. Certain cartoons have been found to present aggression in a funny way that often misleads children into thinking it's okay to hit each other. As parents it is important to educate children that any kind of violence shown onscreen is unacceptable. There are short animation films which present the concept of abuse in a manner that can be easily understood by children. A child's drawings/doodling/art provides insights into his/her mind and if you see the child drawing people behaving in an aggressive manner or being very sad, it may provide vital clues about any aggressive or anxiety-provoking incident that they are being subjected to.

- **Stories** – Story time is a great way of bonding with your child. There are many children's storybooks that talk about abuse and ways to tackle the same. Reading these books with your child can be very helpful for the child to understand the concept of abuse and also learn ways to prevent it or cope with it. You can use creative storytelling in which you play a game of starting a story and asking the child to add to it.

- **Pretend play** – This is one of the favourite games that children of this age group engage in. Pretend play can also provide insights into the fears and wishes of a child. If you suspect that your child may have witnessed or experienced abuse of any kind, pretend play can help elicit information about the same. It is an effective tool to teach the child how to handle a situation if a person tries to abuse them as well as how and whom to approach for help.

- **The feelings game** – This is a creative way to teach children how to express their emotions. You can make flashcards with different scenarios and ask the child how s/he feels about them. Parents can also keep stickers of emoticons which can be pasted on the picture by the child. Through this game you can teach a child that what feels wrong should be shared with parents/trusted adults. The child can also be taught how to use emotions as a means of asserting him/herself.

- **Circle time** – You can encourage your child's school to start this exercise where children are made to sit in a circle. The teacher then picks a topic and asks the children what they think about it and how they feel the issue can be resolved. Circle time at home can be done as a family activity and can be used to discuss a myriad of topics including abuse.

Children (9 to 17 years)

At this age children start understanding logically and can reason out things. They start thinking of what is good or bad from a societal point of view. The concept of teenage has also undergone a change and starts from the age of ten rather than the traditional thirteen years of age. Children at this stage push for independence from their parents in making decisions and asserting themselves. This is also the age when friends become their go-to people and they start keeping secrets from parents. While communicating with this age group, it is important not to preach or patronize. A parent has to play a dual role of being the disciplinarian and friend. The strategies to effectively communicate with teenagers include:

- **Communicate trust and responsibility** – As parents, it is important to communicate to the child that you trust him/her and believe that s/he is a responsible person. This has to be done in a genuine manner that involves both words and actions. You cannot tell a child that you trust him/her and keep calling his/her friends to know what s/he is up to. This is the first step to establish a good rapport with the child and becomes like an automatic checking mechanism for children when they are tempted to do something that may not be 'right' for them.

- **Limit setting** – This involves setting limits in terms of what is acceptable and what is not. Abuse often occurs in high-risk situations, which may include travelling alone at odd hours, initiating contact with an unknown person on the internet, etc. Tell your children that while you trust them and feel they are responsible, there are certain limits that need to be enforced for their safety. The limits can be set for the time they need to be back home, informing parents about who they are going to meet and boundaries regarding intimacy in romantic relationships. The limits should be mutually agreed upon so that the child will abide by them.

- **Accept mistakes** – Children perceive their parents as role models and try hard to live up to their expectations. If they fall short in any way, they feel a sense of shame that makes them keep things from their parents. Teenagers often get into relationships due to peer pressure, which at times turn out to be abusive emotionally, physically or even sexually. The shame often makes the teen keep the abuse a secret. It is important to let your child know that it's okay to make mistakes while experimenting and that you will always support your child even if s/he makes a mistake. However, it is also important to tell your child that abuse in any form is not okay, even if the other person apologizes after the incident. Encourage the child to talk about mistakes or slip-ups so that you can help her/him cope with the consequences. After some time has passed, discuss what went wrong and how such mistakes can be averted in the future.

- **Roll with the resistance** – Teenagers often rebel against parents and disregard what they may be suggesting. If faced with such a situation, roll with the resistance; do not get into a confrontation with the child. Allow the child to put forth his/her views without disregarding them and then offer your point of view. For instance, you may suggest that the child should not engage with strangers on the internet to avoid falling prey to cyberbullying or any other form of abuse. The child may retort that s/he knows better. Rather than getting into an argument, tell the child that you just want to offer your views on how one can avoid becoming a victim of abuse on the internet and s/he can think over it later. This way the child could be more receptive to information and may even think about what you said and inculcate the checks offered to prevent abuse.

In addition to the above strategies, parents need to be aware of certain red flags, for which they need to consult a doctor and/or mental health professional. Red flags for toddlers and young children include:

(1) The child refusing to go to a particular place or meet a certain person.

(2) Showing excessive anxiety in the form of crying, vomiting, trouble falling asleep or passing urine/stool in clothes (despite being fully trained).

(3) Complaining of pain in the genitals or having unexplained bruises/rashes on the body.

(4) Depicting aggressive situations, blood or genitals in drawings.

The red flags with teenagers include:

(1) Appearing anxious or sad for no reason.

(2) Bruises or experiencing pain in the genitals.

(3) Becoming withdrawn or lying about people/places that they have visited.

(4) Resisting meeting people of a certain gender or becoming fearful or anxious while encountering certain persons.

Apart from using these strategies, it is vital for parents to spend time with their children and encourage them to express their views and emotions freely. The backbone of forging an effective relationship with children and getting them to listen to what parents have to say is dependent on adopting a democratic approach to parenting. This involves treating the child as an equal and providing age-appropriate freedom by encouraging children to be responsible for their choices and follow certain rules. Children who have a positive relationship with their parents are more likely to heed their advice and less likely to fall prey to abuse.

20

Substance Use and Addiction

As children take a step towards adolescence, they push for independence. All of a sudden, they start rebelling about anything and everything. They start relying on peers more than parents, and what the peer group says and does becomes the 'gospel truth'. There is a curiosity about pushing boundaries and indulging in novel experiences. One such experience involves using psychoactive or mind-altering substances, which promise to make them feel less stressed, more confident and 'cool' or socially acceptable.

The most commonly used psychoactive substances by teenagers are inhalants, which constitute volatile solvents like white correction fluid. These are usually breathed through the nose (sniffing) or the mouth (huffing). Other frequently used substances include alcohol and tobacco (which can be smoked, chewed or sniffed). For some teenagers, alcohol, tobacco and inhalants may serve as gateway drugs to harder drugs like cannabis, cocaine, etc.

The cycle of abuse starts by using substances casually or socially and then progressing to using the substance more frequently and experiencing negative physical, emotional and social consequences. Addiction or dependence sets in when one needs to consume the substance in larger quantities for the same effect (tolerance), experiences a physical and psychological craving for it and is unable to control or give it up.

As parents, it is our responsibility to keep our children safe from physical and psychosocial harm. Even if your teenager hasn't tried a substance, it is vital that you have a conversation about it so that s/he is better equipped to handle any situation which tempts or pressures him/her into trying it. There are some ground rules that need to be considered before you have a conversation with your teen about substance use. The first rule is to roll with the resistance or avoid confrontation with the teen when broaching the subject of substance use. If your teenager has tried a smoke or alcohol, confronting or shaming will only lead to him/her hiding information from you or rebelling. Communicate in a manner that encourages the teen to consider an alternative perspective. The second rule is to use open-ended questions such as 'what's your take on children and teens trying a smoke or alcohol?' This ensures a non-threatening environment for the teen to freely express what s/he may be feeling or experiencing. The third rule is to use affirmative statements like 'thanks for sharing this with me'. These statements help to build rapport and encourage the teen to reflect on his/her behaviour. The fourth rule is to use reflective listening or paraphrasing the concerns and feelings shared by the teen, for instance, 'So you were feeling angry when your friends were pressuring you to take a puff at that party.' Reflecting a person's beliefs and thoughts is a great way to gain his/her trust and motivate him/her. The final rule is to summarize the main points at the end of a conversation to drive the point home.

Being mindful of the rules mentioned above, the acronym FRAMES describes the steps to talk to a teenager about substance use and motivate him/her to change the patterns of use:

Step 1 – Feedback
The best way to initiate a conversation when you want the full attention of your teenager is to tell him/her that you would like to talk about something important

at a time that is mutually convenient. If you suddenly corner a teenager and initiate a conversation, s/he may approach it with the intention of getting over with it without feeling invested in the process. The feedback step involves initiating a dialogue on what the teenager knows about substance use and what is his/her take on it. Once you get him/her talking, you can supplement information on substance use and risk situations like parties, peer pressure, etc. You can also use examples from your student life where you may have tried a smoke or drink out of curiosity or wanting to be a part of the pack. Following through with the conversation about substance use and risk situations encourages the teen to come up with what s/he perceives could be the advantages and disadvantages of using a substance and which substances does s/he perceive to be safe to use socially. The process of listing the advantages and disadvantages of consuming substances helps to highlight that the benefits are few and short-lived while the repercussions are harmful and have a long-lasting impact on one's health, academics/job, money and social life. Even if the teen may be concealing information and using substances privately, by this simple exercise the seed of reflecting upon his/her actions is sown and maybe at a later time s/he may think about becoming more responsible. When teens are in risk situations, they may not be aware of the negative consequences or may choose to turn a blind eye, but when they are encouraged to think about the same in a non-threatening way, they may use the wisdom to restrain themselves if a similar situation arises in the future.

Step 2 – Responsibility

After discussing the teen's perceptions on substance use, enlisting the possible benefits and harms and supplementing this with more factual information, the next step involves communicating a sense of trust and responsibility. To communicate trust and responsibility, parents need to walk the talk. Come up with ground rules that are mutually agreed upon and tell the teen that you believe s/he is capable of being responsible and mindful of the consequences of his/her actions.

Step 3 – Advice and menu of options

Just providing information about substance use and communicating a sense of trust and responsibility is not enough. It is important to equip the teenager with ways to overcome the temptations and pressures of using substances. The menu of options that can be provided to them include:

(a) Avoiding risk situations – If the teen knows that a certain party will have alcohol or other substances or have certain peers who are likely to pressure him/her into trying out a substance, s/he can give that party a miss by coming up with an excuse.

(b) Positive peer group – Encourage the teen to avoid being alone and have two to three close friends who are a positive influence and can prevent him/her from getting pressurized. Having a positive peer group instils a sense of belonging and emotional security which helps against developing self-destructive habits.

(c) Problem-solving skills – There can be various ways to resolve an issue. Help the teen to brainstorm about ways in which s/he can deal with risk situations or overcome peer pressure, and practise the most practical and appropriate solution.

(d) Assertiveness – Practising communicating in a way which puts across one's thoughts and feelings in a respectful, non-aggressive and non-submissive manner can help in overcoming peer pressure. Practise assertiveness by engaging in role play with the teen to come up with various retorts to resist peer pressure.

(e) Decision-balancing – Every action has pros and cons. Listing these helps to be mindful of the risks that may be involved and can propel the teen to make an informed decision about using a substance.

(f) Challenging negative thoughts – The fear of missing out is something everyone struggles with these days and is one of the reasons which pushes teens to engage in risky behaviour. Making a list of what is the best that can happen, what is the worst that can happen and what is likely is a great way to challenge such fears and negative thoughts. For instance, if you refuse a smoke, what's the best that can happen? Your peers respect your choice and you feel better about refusing it. What's the worst that can happen? They heckle you and call you a sissy and you feel really bad. What's likely to happen? They may tease you for a day or so but will move on and you may feel a little uneasy for some time but will learn to be assertive.

Step 4 – Empathy

While talking to your child, it is vital that you resist the urge to be judgemental and critical. The best way to get children and adolescents to communicate and cooperate is to be empathetic to their points of view and communicate with them in a manner which reflects that you understand their feelings. In case your teen confides in you about using certain substances, communicate that while you may not be in his/her situation, you can gauge that it must be hard to feel vulnerable and be pressured into trying a substance, and that you are glad that s/he chose to talk to you about it. For a teen not using a substance, you can communicate empathy by discussing the various stressors that plague teens today or the fact that standing up to pressures is challenging at times. You can add that despite the fact that you may not be available all the time, you are still accessible if s/he needs help or advice. Using reflective listening and summarizing discussed in the earlier sections is a great way to communicate empathy.

Step 5 – Support self-efficacy

Just like starting a conversation on a positive note is important, it is vital to close it on a similar note as well. After having a conversation about substance use and discussing the ways in which the teen can resist and overcome the urge to use alcohol and other substances, reinforce your confidence in his/her abilities. You can state that just like s/he is good at handling so many other things efficiently, s/he will be able to stay clear of substance use as well. In addition to supporting self-efficacy, reiterate that you are always accessible to help him/her as a sounding board and would be willing to help him/her handle situations which seem overwhelming.

While talking about substance use is important, it is also vital that parents keep their eyes and ears open to notice red flags which may suggest that the child needs professional help. These warning signs are excessive absenteeism or decline in academic performance at school, sudden deterioration of friendships, being evasive or secretive, bloodshot/red eyes, small blue spots/ bruises on the skin, constant runny nose and throat irritation, poor coordination – bumping into things or getting into accidents, sudden mood changes, feeling tired most of the time or hyper-excitability, engaging in stealing/excessive borrowing of money and lying about small things.

Parenting teenagers is more complicated than parenting children, so it's important to maintain a balance between being a parent and a friend to them. Remember that you can get much more with negotiation than confrontation.

21

5 Ways to Develop a Positive Body Image

If the story of Snow White were to be rewritten in the present times, there would be a smart screen instead of the mirror and the queen would ask, 'Social media all around, who is the fairest of them all?' She would go on to compete with Snow White on the number of views and likes. Body image has always been one of the aspects which influences an individual's self-esteem and self-worth. We seek to look and be perceived in a certain way so as to gain acceptance from society at large. Instead of looking within, we conform to the societal standards of beauty, intellect and personality.

Each individual is unique and has a set of attributes which constitute his/her real or actual self. The attributes which s/he admires in others and wishes to incorporate in his/her life constitute the ideal self. When there is a congruence or alignment between these two selves, it fosters mental well-being and self-worth, but when there is a dissonance between the two it may lead to mental distress or poor self-esteem. For instance, in the context of body image, if a person has dusky skin but keeps aspiring to have a fair complexion, there is incongruence between the real and ideal self.

The media at large constantly fuels this incongruence between the real and ideal self and fosters a sense of inadequacy and anxiety on a daily basis. Whether it is advertisements celebrating fair women, or challenges pertaining to altering one's lips to look like those of a celebrity – they all promote a false normal for children, adolescents and adults alike. This comes at a huge physical and emotional cost for many. For instance, adolescent girls who seek tiny waists may go on fad diets and end up with nutritional deficiencies, early osteoporosis, mood swings and eating disorders. As parents, we cannot shield our children from external influences, but we can help them develop more congruence between the real and ideal self.

Here are five ways in which you can ensure that your child develops a positive body image:

1. Introduce the concept

The first step to inculcate any concept is to talk about it, and body image is no different. A healthy body image constitutes feeling satisfied with your body and how you look. For certain parameters like height and weight there are charts which show what is healthy and what is not, but with other attributes like skin colour and facial features there is no healthy standard. Aspiring for a certain weight range may be healthy, but feeling insecure about not being fair or looking a certain way may damage one's self-esteem. For younger children, stories and art are a great way to engage with the child. With stories from different cultures and authors being accessible as e-books and in print, parents are not restricted to narrating the age-old fairy tales that celebrate only fair maidens. Make sure that you introduce your children to different characters with different physical attributes – whether it is via print, animation or even dolls.

Tell your children that just like it's important to eat healthy and exercise, it is important to be happy with the way one looks as well. With adolescents, it is important to discuss the whole emphasis on beauty and body. If you find your teenager idolizing a celebrity for having the perfect body/skin and following fad diets, highlight that the media has tools to enhance features and edit body shapes to make them more attractive. Teenagers at times lack insight that celebrities have an army of experts at their beck and call to make them look the way they do.

There are documentaries and articles available on healthy body types and also on how the beauty industry is vying to make people feel insecure. These can help sow the seed of reflection in the teenager's mind without pressuring him/her.

2. Walk the talk

Talking about body image is half the job. As parents if we are dissatisfied with the way we look and feel, the idea will percolate down to the children as well. At times we may talk to our friends about how fat we have become while the child is in the background, or use fairness creams or restrict our diets despite encouraging the teenager to embrace the way s/he looks. Such things do not go unnoticed and just like the child aspires to be more like the parent to gain acceptance, s/he starts vicariously adopting self-damaging behaviour. Some parents may compare their children and constantly nag a child for being overweight or not looking a certain way. The first step is to become aware of your own patterns and strive to change them.

A simple strategy to recalibrate from self-loathe to self-love is to develop a positive focus. Start your day by thinking of one physical attribute that you like about yourself. It can be an activity that you do with your child in front of the mirror so that they learn to start the day with looking for positives rather than counting the flaws. Make sure that you notice and appreciate the positive qualities of your child on a daily basis and communicate them to foster a positive body image and self-esteem.

3. **Countering body shaming**

Most people have been victims of body shaming at some point in their lives. With the virtual world and social media becoming the point of reference for children and adolescents, it is vital to equip them with tools to counter the ills of social media, which include responding to trolls and body shamers online. The best ways to counter body shaming are:

(a) **Challenge the negative beliefs** – The first step to countering body shaming or negative thoughts about one's body is to test the validity of the negative belief. Tabulating the points of evidence for and against the belief can help do this. Parents can demonstrate and support the child/adolescent while tabulating the evidence.

If the belief is valid, then ask whether you can do something about it or not. If nothing can be done, write the belief on a paper and throw it in the bin. Do this a few times, till you can trash it on a thought level.

(b) **Problem-solving** – If the belief is valid and you can do something about it, brainstorm about all the viable solutions and try out the most practical one to resolve the issue. If it works then keep doing it, or else choose another solution. For instance, you may be overweight as per the health chart for your age and gender and wish to lose weight. For this, you can come up with various solutions like dieting, exercising, avoiding junk food, consulting a nutritionist, etc. Choose the most viable option based on whether it is healthy, and you can follow through with it and see if it is helping you in achieving your goal.

(c) **Assertiveness** – This involves putting forward your viewpoint in an even tone without being disrespectful to the other. As parents, you can engage in role play with your children to come up with counters which can be communicated to body shamers. Alternatively, you can make a game of it by encouraging family members to make slips of situations involving body shaming, and pick the slip and respond to it in as many ways as possible.

4. **Balance the virtual and real world**

Having a routine which maintains a healthy balance between the time spent on the screen and doing regular activities is critical to keep negative beliefs at bay. Make sure that your child has a healthy mix of household chores/daily responsibilities, academic tasks, exercise and screen time so that s/he doesn't spend too much time browsing and obsessing over physical attributes glorified on social media. Supervising the sites that your child/adolescent has access to is equally important to get an insight into what s/he is reading and thinking about. For younger children, parental controls can be placed to view age-appropriate and positive material. For teenagers, it is important to talk to them about how media and social media can influence the way we think and feel about ourselves. Instead of being invasive and spying on the teenagers, encourage open communication so that they can confide in you about their insecurities. In case you feel s/he is being too secretive, talk to a tech person to get access into the sites they may be spending too much time on.

5. **Holistic self-perception**

The self is made up of many aspects and the body/physical attributes is just one of them. You can tell your young child that just like a rainbow has so many colours which make it beautiful, we have many aspects/powers that make us beautiful. Get children to list all the things they like about themselves and focus on different aspects so that they don't hinge the concept of happiness on select attributes. For teenagers and adults, you can make a pie chart of the various aspects which add to your happiness and allocate their importance by putting a percentage/rating for each. List out the attributes/qualities in each domain so it is clear that physical attributes are only a fraction of you and your life. You can also get the child/adolescent to put up a list of the qualities that they possess at a visible place like a pinboard, which they can see every day so as to feel positive about themselves as a whole.

If you notice your child/teenager being too critical of the way s/he looks, constantly trying to lose weight even though s/he is within the average range, bingeing and throwing up after meals, refusing to eat or resorting to unhealthy diets, consult a mental health professional.

Remember, nobody is perfect – whether it is from the perspective of mental or physical attributes. Bodies, physical appearance and societal constructs of beauty will keep changing over the years but a positive attitude about oneself lasts a lifetime.

22

Talking About Relationships and Intimacy with Teens

From an early age children are introduced to the concept of relationships and love through stories. Fairy tales with damsels or princesses and Prince Charming portray the utopian concept of a happily ever after. As your child steps into teenage, s/he seeks out relationships and intimacy for various reasons that include curiosity, need for belonging or peer pressure.

Experiences during dating and establishing romantic relationships have a profound impact on a teen's self-concept and well-being. Positive experiences may provide the teen with a sense of social competence, increased self-esteem, positive self-image and popularity among peer groups. However, negative experiences may lead to stress, poor academic performance, abuse, sexual health concerns, unplanned pregnancies and, at times, depression and self-harm.

With teens being vulnerable to virtual dangers, it is vital that parents go beyond the usual sex education talk and discuss various concerns pertaining to intimacy and relationships. It is essential that these conversations are not one-sided and preachy. Broach the topic with your teen with an intention of having an open discussion and if s/he resists, come back to it later or involve a trusted relative or friend whom the teenager is comfortable with. The discussion regarding concerns doesn't need to be covered all at once and can be paced over time.

The main concerns that need to be discussed and addressed with teens include:

1. Healthy and unhealthy relationships

The first step to talking about relationships and intimacy is to get an understanding of what these mean to your child.

Encourage the teen to talk about the reasons and benefits of dating and seeking relationships. Additionally, you can discuss healthy and unhealthy relationships. While explaining healthy relationships, make a circle on a paper and divide it into segments. Ask your teen to imagine it as a pizza or a pie. Now present two scenarios of eating the whole pie/pizza at once or one slice at a time, and ask which one would be more pleasant or enjoyable. When the teen picks the slice scenario tell him/her that just like eating a slice is better than eating the whole at once, dividing our life into different domains (family, relationship, friends, academics, etc.) rather than having one aspect becoming the sole focus is a healthier and balanced way to lead one's life. This approach also helps in not feeling shattered if a relationship doesn't work out.

Healthy relationships help partners grow personally and in other spheres of life, and are underscored by mutual trust and respect.

The concept of unhealthy relationships can be explained by highlighting the red flags, which include:

(1) Lying about trivial things from time to time.
(2) Cheating on your partner.
(3) Emotionally blackmailing or pressurizing to do things which the other may not be comfortable with.
(4) Using abuses or showing disrespect for one's partner (or friends and family).
(5) Hitting or causing physical harm.

(6) Displaying self-destructive behaviour patterns (binge-drinking, substance use, resorting to self-harm).

(7) Being possessive and intrusive (asking one's partner not to talk to certain friends, checking personal mails/messages, etc.).

(8) Sharing personal/intimate messages with others without consent.

The teen can be encouraged to talk to a parent or a trusted adult if s/he encounters any of the above red flags in a relationship, so that s/he can be helped to put an end to the relationship in a safe manner.

2. Real and virtual relationships

In the era of dating apps and social media, it is vital to ensure that the teen doesn't get involved with persons who can exploit him/her.

Explain to the teen that while social media and dating apps seem to provide more opportunities of meeting people, they may not be the safest mediums to date or pursue relationships. Rather than lecturing the teen, encourage him/her to talk about the potential threats while seeking a partner on a dating app or social media. Supplement the threats highlighted by the teen with additional information.

It could be a good idea to have a trusted relative or friend who has a good knowledge of technology while discussing the topic to add credibility to the concerns. For dating and pursuing relationships in the real world, it is important to caution the teen against getting involved with unknown persons.

Monitoring social media use by the teen and ensuring that s/he is not using apps for which the age criterion is more than the teen's age is essential. You can also watch documentaries or short films with your teen about sexual grooming in the real and virtual worlds, sugar daddies, dangers of sharing personal information on the web or dating frauds to educate him/her about potential threats.

As you make the teen aware of these dangers, make sure that you do not create a grim picture of dating and relationships.

3. **Establishing boundaries**

Boundaries are an important aspect of any relationship.

You can do an activity that explains the concept of boundaries with your teen. Draw a circle in the middle of a blank page, and then draw one around it and another one around that. Label the first one as the innermost circle and ask the teen to write down the names of people whom s/he considers very close. Now label the circle around it as the middle circle, which has persons whom one may interact with on a regular basis but may not be emotionally close to. The third or outermost circle consists of acquaintances. Explain to the teen that when we date someone, they are in the outermost circle, and as one gets to know a person over time and moves towards a relationship, the person too moves from the outermost to the innermost circle. Similarly, one should enforce boundaries depending on the circle the person is in. For instance, getting physically intimate or sharing intimate information with a person who is an acquaintance may not be wise.

Boundaries also apply to teens in terms of having curfews for going out, and knowing where and who s/he is with. A mutual understanding between the parent and teen about what is okay and what is not is important. Do not keep calling frequently to check on the teen or reprimand him/her about meeting someone you do not approve of. Instead, set a time to connect with him/her and discuss your reservations without being dismissive.

The concept of consent is closely related to boundaries, and the teen should be made aware that the law prohibits consensual sexual activity if you are under the age of eighteen. This is particularly relevant, as at times teens may engage in consensual sex without understanding its consequences – physical, emotional and legal.

4. **Rejection, hook-ups, break-ups and rebounds**
   While discussing relationships and intimacy, it is also important to discuss associated scenarios.

   Before dating, teens may face scenarios where they like someone but s/he may not feel the same way or a date may not translate into anything more. Similarly, at times one may reject another's advances, which may not go down well with the other person and s/he may create unpleasantness as a result. Whether a teen is facing such a scenario or the concern is brought up independently, point out that there may be instances where we are attracted to someone but s/he may not feel the same way, or we may think a date went well but it may not meet the other's expectations. In those circumstances, instead of personalizing the rejection and feeling that you are not good enough, focus on the fact that there are friends who appreciate you the way you are, and one or even a few rejections do not suggest that you will never meet someone who appreciates you.

   If the teen rejects someone's advances and the

person is creating unpleasantness, suggest ways to cope with it or intervene as a parent if need be. While discussing hook-ups, it is important to address peer pressure that may compel one to get intimate with someone as a way of looking cool or being accepted in the group. Explain to the teen that while something may look cool, it may not feel right, and that one can always assert oneself and say no if something is not appealing. While hooking up with someone, it is important to weigh the possible consequences as well to make an informed decision.

Break-ups should be seen as a part of the relationship experience and should not be taken as a 'personal failing'. If a teen is going through a break-up, be supportive instead of being critical. Ensure that s/he is surrounded by friends and family members who can help her/him through the process. Be alert if s/he talks about or attempts self-harm and seek professional help.

Allow the teen time to grieve about the loss of the relationship, but caution about resorting to rebounds as a means to get over the estranged partner. Encourage the teen to take three to six months off instead to focus on other things/experiences so that one does not take any emotional baggage of a previous relationship into the new one.

While talking about intimacy and relationships, it is important for parents to reflect on their own relationships as well since children imbibe the behaviour and dynamic followed at home. For instance, if a girl grows up seeing the father abuse and hit the mother, and the mother accepting and normalizing it, she may think it is acceptable to be abused or hit by a partner. Equality in relationships needs to be reflected in parental relationships for it to be mirrored in the teen's future relationships. Parents need to sensitize teens that they should not deliberately hurt someone or cause harm to another while pursuing a relationship.

Remember that despite making teens aware of all aspects of intimacy and relationships, they may still falter and not pay heed to sensibilities. At such times, it is important to help the teen reflect on his/her actions so s/he can learn from the situation rather than be overcritical and close the doors of honest communication. If you notice that your child has been crying a lot, lying, has unexplained bruises or cuts, using substances, or behaving in a manner that is unlike him/her after getting into a relationship or while going through a break-up, try to talk to him/her about it but if you are not able to get through, seek professional help.

23

Positive Thinking for Young Adults

Just like superheroes have a superpower that helps them feel good and help others, we also have a superpower – the power of positive thinking.

The art of positive thinking can have a profound impact on the way children, adolescents and young adults feel about and respond to situations and people around them. As parents, we all strive to think positively ourselves and impart the skill to our children. However, most of us are on an autopilot mode of 'flaw-focused parenting'. This involves paying more attention to the mistakes that the child makes or the tasks that s/he struggles to perform. This approach fosters a 'negative focus' in perception and thought, due to which children and adolescents grow up focusing more on 'what's wrong' and 'what needs to be fixed' rather than 'what's working well' and 'what can be built upon'.

The first step to fostering positive thinking is to break away from the 'flaw-focused approach' and embrace the 'ability-focused approach'. The ability-focused approach offers appreciation to the child for the tasks that s/he is able to perform well, while encouraging the child to improve upon the ones that need attention. Balancing criticism and appreciation and providing concrete steps for improvement have a positive impact on the child's self-worth and self-esteem. The second step towards inculcating positive thinking involves 'managing negative thoughts'. Negative thoughts have an inherent value, as they serve as an 'alert' system for something that needs attention. Substituting or superimposing negative thoughts with positive thoughts is superficial and serves as a short-lived distraction. Repressing negative thoughts is like brushing dirt under the carpet and pretending that the room is clean. Repressed negative thoughts constantly seek expression and lead to anxiety, frustration and sadness.

The following techniques can help manage negative thoughts effectively and sustain positive thinking:

1. **Focus on the 'what' and not the 'why'**

    Most people have a tendency to react and respond to every negative thought that crops up by getting entangled with the 'why did this thought occur?'

instead of thinking 'what can I do about it?' The answer to the 'why' may not be available at times, particularly if it is in relation to the way another person has reacted or due to a reason that may be beyond one's comprehension. However, the 'what' can be addressed via the 'problem-solving approach'. This approach involves clearly stating the negative thought, brainstorming about the possible solutions, weighing the pros and cons by anticipating the consequences for each solution and following through with the most viable option. Coming up with a solution or plan of action makes one feel more in control of a situation and helps to positively cope with negative thoughts.

2. **Ignore and use active distraction**

There are many negative thoughts which may be irrational. Instead of paying attention to these thoughts and getting disturbed by them, one can ignore them by active distraction. Active distraction refers to engaging in an activity that will take one's focus away from the negative thought. Each person can come up with a list of distractors such as talking to a friend, listening to a song/music, etc. to serve as a ready reckoner for ignoring negative thoughts. Another way to ignore negative thoughts that are non-addressable is to write them down on a piece of paper, crumple it and throw it in the bin. In this way, over time the mind becomes adept at distinguishing between addressable and non-addressable thoughts and trashes the non-addressable ones automatically.

3. **Set aside a 'worry hour'**
   Most negative thoughts work on the principle of instant gratification and keep disturbing a person till a resolution is reached. This may be particularly distressing when one is engaged in an important work or personal tasks during the day. Setting aside a specific time every day as 'worry hour' and thinking about all types of anxiety-provoking thoughts at that time helps to slot negative thoughts and exercise control over them. Constant worrying about certain things leads to a state of mental exhaustion, where one cannot worry any more. This leads to a decrease in the frequency of negative thoughts over time and instils a sense of mastery or positivity.

4. **Create gratitude and ability lists**
   People usually start and end their day with anxiety-provoking thoughts by dissecting the activities planned for the day down to the very last detail. As they do so, they tend to focus on their mistakes

and on the tasks that could not be completed. This sets the tone for a series of negative thoughts throughout the day. This negative cycle can be broken if we start and end the day by recounting 'one thing' that we are grateful for and 'one ability' that we possess, as it helps to shift our mental focus from negative to positive. Older children and adolescents can be encouraged to write these in a journal or pin them up on a board and use them as a daily positivity booster.

5. **Use disputation**

There are certain common types of 'errors in thinking' that form the basis of most negative thoughts. These include 'all or none' thinking, 'maximizing and minimizing', 'mind reading', 'overgeneralization' and 'labelling'. All or none thinking refers to thinking in polarities as 'good' or 'bad'. For instance, if a child is not able to get 90 per cent in her/his examinations, s/he feels like a failure. Maximizing and minimizing is about giving importance to the negative aspects and downplaying the positive aspects of one's life. Mind reading refers to constantly worrying about what others will think or feel. Overgeneralization is jumping to conclusions based on one negative experience. Labelling refers to attaching negative labels like 'loser', 'failure', etc. to oneself. These errors in thinking cause undue distress and affect one's self-esteem. Using the disputation strategy can help to counter these errors. Disputation involves coming up with points or listing the evidence against the negative thought. Once disputed, the thought loses its validity and ability to disturb a person.

6. **Evaluate the best/worst/likely scenarios**

One negative thought often triggers another and then a host of others, creating a domino effect that leads young adults to anticipate worst-case scenarios. Writing down the best, worst and likely consequences/scenarios helps one to put things in perspective and think rationally. It also helps one realize that the likely consequences are never as bad as the feared worst-case scenarios and can be addressed via problem-solving or disputation strategies.

7. **Make a 'negative thought box'**

This technique seeks to combine the worry hour, problem-solving and disputation techniques into a cohesive whole. The young adult can be encouraged to write down the negative thoughts that s/he experiences during the day and put them in a specific box. A specific time can be set aside on a daily basis to review these thoughts and sift them into 'addressable' and 'non-addressable'. Non-addressable or repetitive thoughts can be crumpled and thrown into the bin and addressable ones can be countered using disputation or problem-solving techniques. Over time the number of thoughts reduces and the efficiency in countering negative thoughts increases, providing the person a sense of control and a positive frame of mind.

8. **Draw a self-chart**

If one aspect of a person's life is not working out, s/he tends to keep thinking about it and the negativity that is attached to that one aspect tends to spill over to all the others as well. To counter this negative bias and feel more positive about oneself and life in general, the young adult can be encouraged to draw a self-chart by making a circle and dividing it into segments. These segments reflect the aspects/domains which provide him/her a sense of happiness and positivity, such as family, friends, academics, interests, etc. After identifying the domains, s/he can identify the aspects that are working well and those that require improvement. Most of the time the majority of the aspects are working well and only one or two need improvement. This simple activity helps to put life in perspective and shifts the mental focus from negative to positive and also helps in taking the necessary steps to turn things around.

9. **Follow a mental diet**

People follow diets to enrich their meals with nutritious food and curb the consumption of junk food to keep their bodies healthy. Similarly, young adults need to follow a 'mental diet' to instil and sustain a positive mindset. This diet entails avoiding watching or reading material that is mentally disturbing and avoiding conversations with people who are negative and critical. Watching inspirational videos and podcasts or reading books that are motivating and positive help in positivity becoming a part of one's subconscious mind. Similarly, surrounding oneself with people who are encouraging and positive helps in vicariously adopting a positive mindset.

It is always a good idea for parents to model the skills and strategies they wish their children to imbibe. Try to pick up one or two strategies, which are easy to understand, and follow through, and then build on them over time. If you notice that despite all your best efforts as a parent the child is struggling with repetitive negative thoughts or feeling hopeless, helpless and worthless, or is having thoughts of harming him/herself, then it is crucial to contact a trained mental health professional and seek help.

Positive thinking should not be considered as the absence of negative thinking. A positive mindset is one which is aware of the negative thoughts that crop up from time to time and focuses on ways to effectively address them.

24

Single Parenting

The concept of families has undergone a change over time. Traditionally, the image of a father, mother and child would flash in our minds when we thought about a 'family'. In the present day, the concept of family is no longer restricted to a married couple with children. There are nuclear families, extended families, single-parent families, step-parent families or blended families, families headed by two unmarried partners – either of the same sex or the opposite sex, adoptive families and families with grandparents or relatives raising children. Single-parent families are the ones in which the family is headed by a parent who is separated or divorced (but not remarried), widowed or single. While every parent faces challenges in parenting his/her children, the challenges of a single parent may be different owing to the fact that s/he is managing work, child-rearing, household chores and finances alone.

While many believe that children of single parents are at a disadvantage as compared to those growing up with two parents, it may not be the true picture. Children of single parents who undergo a significant amount of stress due to parental discord, abuse, financial constraints and parental neglect are at a higher risk of developing emotional and behavioural issues such as anxiety, depression, loneliness, trust issues, poor academic performance, anger outbursts or substance abuse. However, if these issues are addressed in time and efficiently, these children can grow up to be independent, responsible and emotionally secure individuals.

The strategies that can help make single parenting a fulfilling experience are:

Talk about it
Children who may have lost a parent or are in the midst of a divorce may feel helpless and try to make sense of their situation. Instead of just providing children reassurance, talk to them about the fears and feelings they may be nursing as a result of the event. Since older children understand things better than younger ones, you can have a discussion with them and address their

feelings and queries. For younger children, you can use storybooks to make the child understand what happens when a person passes away or why parents are not able to stay together. You can also use examples that they can relate to. For instance, to explain the concept of separation, you can tell the child that in class, when two friends sitting on a table keep fighting, the teacher makes them sit separately till they can learn to get along. In the same manner, mom and dad are fighting a lot and need to stay separately till they feel they can get along. If the child feels s/he is responsible for what has happened, assure her/him that that is not the case. It is very important to address any feelings of guilt that the child may be harbouring.

For the parent who may have adopted a child or had a child through surrogacy, s/he may miss not having another parent or may be taunted by others in class. You can use a creative analogy and tell him/her that some parents have a superpower and they can be both mummy and daddy. You can get them to draw their parent with a superhero's costume and show it to their friends as well. Make sure that you are accessible and encourage the child to talk to you about anything. Open and honest communication sets the tone for trust and helps the child feel emotionally secure.

Encourage and show affection

A child is never too old for a warm hug and words of love. Being a single parent and managing so many fronts at a time may lead to the parent reacting to only instances of negative behaviour and overlooking positive behaviour. This results in the child engaging in negative behaviour more as unconsciously s/he associates it with attention. Instead of only reprimanding negative behaviour, make it a habit to appreciate your child for the little things s/he does and steal a hug whenever you can.

Encouraging positive and prosocial behaviour reinforces it and helps the child link engaging in positive actions to attention. This in turn gives the child a sense of industry or competence and boosts the child's self-confidence. Hugs provide a sense of contact comfort for the child and help him/her feel more secure and loved.

Establish boundaries

At times, the child may manipulate the parent by guilt-tripping a single parent. Hence, it is important to establish clear rules and boundaries of what is acceptable and what is not. Involve the child in coming up with family rules so that s/he feels more invested in the process. In case of separated/divorced parents, it is not necessary that your parenting style be the same as your estranged partner's. Make the child aware that the rules can be different for the other parent but need to be followed. In case of visitation arrangements and custody battles, make sure that you communicate and enforce boundaries with your estranged partner so that you feel more at ease and are able to parent your child effectively.

'Us time'

Set aside some time daily to spend with your child and engage in an activity that s/he would like you to do together. Keep distractions like the phone away during this time. Spending exclusive time at a given hour daily helps in building a positive relationship. If there is more than one child, make sure that you spend exclusive time with each child daily. With older kids and teenagers, you can introduce the concept of a 'problem-solving hour' on weekends, when the teenager can be encouraged to talk about the things that s/he found stressful during the week and you can discuss ways in which these issues can be addressed/resolved. This simple activity helps to acknowledge the teenager's concerns/feelings, keep the channels of communication open and build trust. It is also a great way to inculcate coping skills such as problem-solving, assertiveness, etc.

Support system

You may aspire to be a supermom or superdad but may still have trouble following through with the balancing act. Identify people in your family or friends and acquaintances who can be a part of your daily support system. Make sure to have friends and family whom you can reach out to for emotional support so that you can turn to them whenever you feel stressed or overwhelmed. There may be times when a single parent needs help to address sensitive issues with the child of the opposite sex, for instance, a single father may need the help of a family member or friend who is a mother to speak to his daughter about menstruation or other sensitive topics that she may not want to discuss with her father. Apart from emotional support, there can be some parents from the child's class or parent groups who can help you with carpool or to stay updated with school activities and assignments. Managing children and work can be challenging, so it is vital that you have reliable people who can help supervise the child when you are preoccupied with work and can help with household chores. Apart from having your support system as a parent, it is important to educate the child about it and get him/her to identify family and friends that s/he can rely on apart from you. Make sure that you are aware of your child's friends and acquaintances in the real and virtual worlds.

Plan, prioritize and organize

Having a routine for yourself and your child is important so that you feel more in control and the child is gainfully occupied. Routines give a sense of stability and consistency, which help buffer feelings of helplessness that may surface from time to time. Make sure that the child has a routine with a mix of activities that s/he wants to engage in and some household chores as well which s/he may not like. Avoid overindulging in screen time or overly pampering the child to counter the guilt that you may have for not spending enough time or for putting the child through emotional distress while going through separation or divorce. This will help the child to be more resilient and not a slave to his/her likes and dislikes. Hence, maintaining a balance with limited screen time, prioritizing tasks as per urgency and importance and keeping the welfare of the child above everything else is vital. If there are financial constraints, review your spending heads and see where you can cut back. You could also consult a finance professional to suggest ways in which you can diversify your financial portfolio and ensure that your child's basic needs and education are taken care of.

Self-care

Make sure that you take time out to do things on an individual level. It is important that you prioritize your physical and mental health so that you can effectively parent your child. If you are losing your cool, abusing substances or are distraught, you may end up being more reactive with the child and raise his/her anxiety level. The child may also start emulating your behaviour, which can bring up more issues. Reach out to a family member, friend or a health professional to help you handle emotions better if you aren't able to do so. Realize that there will be certain issues that you will be able to resolve and some that you may not be able to. Focus on the ones which you can do something about by adopting a problem-solving approach of coming up with possible solutions to a given problem and choosing the most viable one. For instance, if you are not getting along with your estranged partner and are not able to co-parent, try to seek help from a trusted friend or professional who can help you both come up with ways in which the child can spend time with and get the best from both parents.

Channelling guilt is very important and can be done by writing down feelings in a journal or on a paper that can be trashed if you don't want anyone to find it. Maintaining a social life and engaging in hobbies which don't involve the child may also help avoid helicopter parenting. If you would like to start dating again, do so but avoid getting the date home to spend time with your child till you feel you are ready to make a commitment with the new partner and have spoken to the child about it. If the child is resistant to meet your partner or is angry with you for seeing someone, talk to him/her and explain that you are not replacing the other parent. Make sure that you communicate to the child that nobody can take his/her place in your heart and life.

If your child is suffering from anxiety, avoiding friends, having crying spells, performing poorly at school, doesn't feel like doing the things that s/he liked, has started bed-wetting or behaving in a childish manner, and despite your best efforts you or people from your support system are not able to help him/her, consult a mental health professional.

Above everything else, be kind to yourself and forgive yourself for the times that you may fail at doing what is best for your child.

Select Bibliography

Anderson, J., and A. Lightfoot (2019). *The School Education System in India: An Overview.* New Delhi: British Council.

Barbor, T.F., and J.C. Higgins-Biddle (2001). 'Brief Intervention for Hazardous and Harmful Drinking: A Manual for Use in Primary Care' (WHO/MSD/MSB/01.6b). Retrieved from the World Health Organization Department of Mental Health and Substance Dependence. http://whqlibdoc.who.int/hq/2001/who_msd_msb_01.6b.pdf

Beck, J.S. (2011). *Cognitive Behavior Therapy: Basics and Beyond* (2nd edn.). Guilford Press.

Berk, L.E. (2013). *Child Development* (9th edn.). Boston, MA: Pearson.

Bloom, H. (2001). *How to Read and Why.* New York: Touchstone.

Bussey, K., and A. Bandura (1999). 'Social Cognitive

Theory of Gender Development and Differentiation'. *Psychological Review*, 106(4): 676–713.

Cash, H., C.D. Rae, A.H. Steel, and A. Winkler (2012). 'Internet Addiction: A Brief Summary of Research and Practice'. *Current Psychiatry Reviews*, 8(4): 292–98. https://doi.org/10.2174/157340012803520513

Ellis, A., and D.J. Ellis (2011). *Rational Emotive Behavior Therapy*. Washington, DC: American Psychological Association.

Franklin, B. (1928). *The Autobiography of Benjamin Franklin*. Boston: Houghton Mifflin Company.

Lal, R., R. Rao, and I. Mohan (2005). *Substance Use Disorder – Manual for Physicians*. New Delhi: All India Institute of Medical Sciences.

Lall, R.M. (2004). *Among the Hindus: A Study of Hindu Festivals*. New Delhi: Asian Educational Services.

Price, C. (2017). The Trophy Child. *Library Journal*, 142(1): 86.

Robertson, E.B., S.L. David, and S.A. Rao (2003). *Preventing Drug Use Among Children and Adolescents: A Research-based Guide for Parents, Educators, and Community Leaders* (2nd edn.). Bethesda, MD: National Institute on Drug Abuse No. 04-4212 (A). Retrieved from http://www.drugabuse.gov/sites/default/files/preventingdruguse.pdf

Ruble, D.N., C. Martin, and S. Berenbaum (2006).

'Gender Development'. *Handbook of Child Psychology (Vol. 3): Personality and Social Development* (6th edn.), edited by N. Eisenberg. New York: Wiley.

Safire, W. (1 May 1994). 'On Language; Trophy Wife'. *The New York Times*, pp. 26.

Samara, M., V. Burbidge, A. El Asam, M. Foody, P.K. Smith, and H. Morsi (2017). 'Bullying and Cyberbullying: Their Legal Status and Use in Psychological Assessment'. *International Journal of Environmental Research and Public Health*, 14(12): 1449. https://doi.org/10.3390/ijerph14121449

Santrock, J.W. (2004). *Educational Psychology* (2nd edn.). New York: McGraw-Hill.

Shanahan, T., K. Callison, C. Carriere, N. K. Duke, P. D. Pearson, C. Schatschneider, and J. Torgesen (2010). *Improving Reading Comprehension in Kindergarten Through 3rd Grade: A Practice Guide* (NCEE 2010-4038). Washington, DC: National Center for Education Evaluation and Regional Assistance, Institute of Education Sciences, U.S. Department of Education.

World Health Organization (2019). *Guidelines on Physical Activity, Sedentary Behavior and Sleep for Children Under 5 Years of Age*. Geneva: WHO Press.

Ziglar, Z. (1975). *See You at the Top*. Gretna: Pelican Publication Company.

Acknowledgements

At first there was an idea, then slowly words followed and finally a coherent narrative came together. I am grateful that I am surrounded by family and friends who were a constant source of encouragement throughout the creative process.

This book is a tribute to my grandparents and parents. I am blessed to have had grandparents who were wonderful storytellers and encouraged creative expression. My parents and brother continue to be my biggest sources of strength and inspiration. They taught me that mistakes and failure should not be feared but seen as opportunities for growth. I appreciate my parents-in-law for giving my talent space to breathe when I started on a new course of life. My husband, Nikhil, deserves special mention for making parenting look easy and for being a hands-on father to our children. His unflinching emotional support has helped

Acknowledgements

me tide over many a writer's block. I am grateful to my children, Kabir and Mira, for their warm hugs which help me start and end each day with a smile.

I am deeply indebted to my teacher Dr Sangeeta Bhatia, who always encouraged me to believe in my abilities and has been the wind beneath my wings. I am thankful to my cousin Gauri and my friends Tanushree and Garima for always being there for me and being sounding boards to bounce off ideas.

Last but not least, this book would not have been possible without the support of Chiki Sarkar and her talented team at Juggernaut Books. My editor Ananya Saha deserves special mention for believing in my vision of parenting and for smoothening the rough edges.

A Note on the Author

A mother of two, Dr Anubha Majithia is a practising clinical psychologist. She has a PhD from the All India Institute of Medical Sciences (AIIMS), New Delhi. She has previously worked on a multi-country World Health Organization (WHO) project to develop a portal for managing alcohol use (https://www.alcoholwebindia. in). She has also worked in the public health sector on a project for school health funded by the Michael and Susan Dell Foundation.

When she isn't helping people solve their problems, she loves to get lost in a museum or an art gallery.

CRAFTED FOR MOBILE READING

Thought you would never read a book on mobile? Let us prove you wrong.

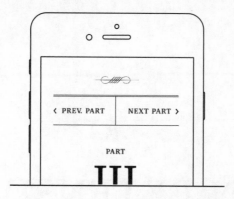

Beautiful Typography

The quality of print transferred
to your mobile. Forget ugly PDFs.

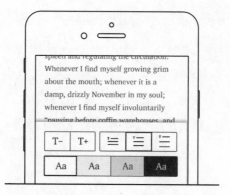

Customizable Reading

Read in the font size, spacing
and background of your liking.

AN EXTENSIVE LIBRARY

Including fresh, new, original Juggernaut books from the likes of Sunny Leone, Praveen Swami, Husain Haqqani, Umera Ahmed, Rujuta Diwekar and lots more. Plus, books from partner publishers and loads of free classics. Whichever genre you like, there's a book waiting for you.

DON'T JUST READ; INTERACT

We're changing the reading experience from passive to active.

Ask authors questions

Get all your answers from the horse's mouth.
Juggernaut authors actually reply to every
question they can.

Rate and review

Let everyone know of your favourite reads or
critique the finer points of a book – you will be
heard in a community of like-minded readers.

Gift books to friends

For a book-lover, there's no nicer gift than
a book personally picked. You can even
do it anonymously if you like.

Enjoy new book formats

Discover serials released in parts over
time, picture books including comics,
and story-bundles at discounted rates.
And coming soon, audiobooks.

LOWEST PRICES & ONE-TAP BUYING

Books start at ₹10 with regular discounts and free previews.

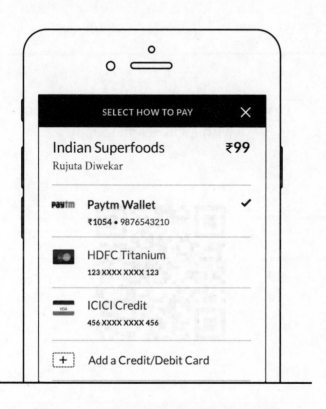

Paytm Wallet, Cards & Apple Payments

On Android, just add a Paytm Wallet once and buy any book with one tap. On iOS, pay with one tap with your iTunes-linked debit/credit card.

To download the app scan the QR Code
with a QR scanner app

For our complete catalogue, visit www.juggernaut.in
To submit your book, send a synopsis and two
sample chapters to books@juggernaut.in
For all other queries, write to contact@juggernaut.in